Balancing God, Science, *and* Technology *in the* End-Times

JUANITA WERRETT

ISBN 978-1-0980-6965-0 (paperback)
ISBN 978-1-0980-6966-7 (digital)

Christian Faith Publishing, Inc.
832 Park Avenue
Meadville, PA 16335
www.christianfaithpublishing.com

Printed in the United States of America

Contents

Author's Notes
Goals and Purposes

My name is Juanita Werrett. I am a grandmother on a mission. I have held a deep interest in the religious study of the Gospel of Christ throughout my life. I am a student and teacher of the Bible, the prophets—ancient and modern—and the standard works of the Church of Jesus Christ of Latter-day Saints.

In 2016, I embarked on a new and, for me, an unusual science study that synchronized with my gospel knowledge. I jumped feet first into a challenging study of quantum particle physics. That may seem like a strange direction to take, but I have always known our Heavenly Father is the source of all spiritual and scientific laws that govern His cosmos.

My desire is to honor and reverence Heavenly Father with full purpose of heart. Through my life experiences, I have come to recognize that God has a very subtle and endearing sense of humor.

I am musing over this strange juxtaposition, as a grandma on one hand and a deep dive study into particle physics and technology. I think both God and I have chuckled at this thought more than once. However, I think He and I know the urgency of sharing this knowledge.

This information weighs heavy on me, but the weight will be greater if I don't share it.

Science has always danced in the background of my Gospel study. This current study was so powerful and tantalizing that it took me captive; my excitement has spilled over onto my devoted husband who shares my interest and willingly supports my efforts. He is my champion, who adores and endures me.

As I began to understand the basic mechanics and relationship of modern telecommunication technology and physics, it struck me that this is a marriage made in heaven. This marriage has a family that includes quantum computing, particle accelerators, artificial intelligence, inter-dimensional powers, blockchain, 5G systems, virtual realities, and many other offspring.

Early on, the spiritual and intuitive parts of my nature recognized a foreboding danger in this scientific technology surge. Even now, three years into my study, I hold equal levels of fear and exhilaration about the quantum-technology mix.

Often, this knowledge is a burden, and often this burden of awareness is weighted with urgency to warn others. Even the watchmen on the high walls of Israel were tasked to warn the populace when their enemies were approaching. As one small voice, I can no longer ignore newfound scientific truths and their implications for humanity. So I am raising a warning to those who will listen.

The exponential forward strides of this new technology will overtake all of us like a tsunami. It is in motion, and it is my considered opinion that three main areas of the new science working in tandem will hasten the end-time scenario leading to the "system of the beast." This system is one of surveillance and control that could possibly lead to stealing of freewill and deadening the souls of mankind. Satan's original campaign was to usurp the agency of God's children. Satan would stamp out individualism and freedom to choose.

These worrisome dangers of tyrannical control are being birthed in the discovery of: (a) the new D-Wave quantum computers, which support the experiments taking place at, (b) the Large Hadron Particle Collider near Geneva, Switzerland (CERN), and (c) the digitizing of human DNA.

My goal is to share the information I have discovered and relay the inevitable outcomes that are currently affecting all world populations.

As individual awareness of this new technology increases, astute people will be awakened to the threat. As you get acquainted with the message of this book, you may experience the same uneasiness I feel.

In regards to your new understanding of quantum technology, you may ask, "Should I fear or embrace?" "Should I reject or accept?" "Is this science benevolent or malevolent?" "Does this system offer independence or control?" "Will it lead to freedom or tyranny?" Will we experience the non-centralized platforms that have been promised or will the power brokers in government, science, and industry insist on full centralized control?

Any or all of those responses are possible, but none of them are really negotiable. The technology is here and moving forward at warp speed.

What really does matter are the origins and goals of these foundational scientific breakthroughs. We must pay heed to the genesis of these synergistic forces powering our science and technology.

Forecasters are touting the profit motive in this new combination of technology. Combined with the hundreds of spin-off companies will top out above $17 trillion in profits.

Nothing can stop this technology juggernaut.

Remember, you can buy anything in this world for money, or maybe you can buy anything in this world for digitized cryptocurrency.

Author Credits

As I close my book writing experience, I wish to give heartfelt accolades to the true authors who have richly contributed to my understanding of the world of science, technology, and especially religion. I am not a scientist or an editor. But I am a devoted Christian, fact finder, and reporter. The following list presents treasured books that supported and enriched my study. I recommend any or all of these books for your enjoyment and learning.

Recommended Books

Standard works of the Church of Jesus Christ of Latter-day Saints:

Holy Bible: Old and New Testaments.

Book of Mormon. These records originated with the Jewish prophet Lehi, a contemporary of Jeremiah who was warned of God to gather his family and leave Jerusalem. He was instructed to leave his home and travel into the desert prior to the devastating attack of the Babylonians. King Nebuchadnezzar besieged Jerusalem in 605 BCE. The Lehi family journey brought them across the ocean and to the American continent.

The *Book of Mormon* is another testament of Jesus Christ and is similar to the Bible in that it is a collection of the writings of prophets who, while describing activities of their day, are mainly testifying of Jesus Christ as the Messiah. The *Book of Mormon* takes place in the ancient Americas and is a compilation of spiritual and historical records written by prophets, just as the Bible is. The crowning event recorded in the *Book of Mormon* is the account of the resurrected Lord Jesus Christ ministering, teaching, and blessing people in the Americas. The *Book of Mormon* is actually a collection of histories passed down from Lehi to consecutive prophets over many years. Each author always gave the record to someone they trusted. After hundreds of years, the record was given to Mormon, who condensed all the writings into one volume, engraved on thin sheets of metal. He titled it the *Book of Mormon*. Before he died, Mormon passed the plates to his son, Moroni. Moroni added a few words and then buried the plates. These great nations were destroyed by idolatry, wickedness, and war. Archeologists are finding evidence of their existence.

In 1823, Moroni appeared to Joseph Smith as an angel and told him where the plates were buried. Joseph Smith translated the plates into English by the gift and power of God, and the *Book of Mormon* was published in Palmyra, New York, in 1830. Since that time, this sacred volume has been translated into more than a hundred languages, and over 150 million copies have appeared in print.

The Pearl of Great Price. Within this volume are choice selections of revelations, translations, and narrations of the Prophet Joseph Smith. It contains the Book of Moses, the enriched Pentateuch, which are the first five books of the Old Testament. This volume also includes translations from a papyrus record taken from the catacombs of Egypt preserved by the Lord. This volume is titled the Book of Abraham. Abraham was the original author. This book contains priceless information, which is not available in any other writings. The Book of Abraham is a work produced between 1835 and 1842 by Joseph Smith. The book originated with Egyptian papyri that Joseph Smith translated beginning in 1835.

Doctrine and Covenants. This volume contains the ongoing revelations through 1844 of Joseph Smith, the founder and president of the Church of Jesus Christ of Latter-day Saints. Many sections of the D&C came to Joseph Smith by direct revelation. This book is specifically revealed for followers of Christ living today. This volume holds the words of God spoken to modern man through a modern prophet.

- *Revising Reality: A Biblical Look into the Cosmos*, Anthony Patch, Josh Peck Conzo Shimura, and S. Douglas Woodward
- *The Wise Shall Understand: Daniel And Revelation*, Tom Stapleton
- *The God Code: The Secret of Our Past, the Promise of our Future*, Gregg Braden
- *Under an Ionized Sky: From Chemtrails to Space Fence Lockdown*, Elana Freeland
- *Google Archipelago: The Digital Gulag and the Simulation of Freedom*, Michael Rectenwald
- *The Triumph of Zion: Our Personal Quest for the New Jerusalem*, John M. Pontius
- *Surviving AI: The Promise and Peril of Artificial Intelligence*, Calum Chace
- *Earth in the Beginning*, Eric N. Skousen, PhD
- *Everlasting Burnings*, M. Garfield Cook
- *The Key to Theology*, Parley P. Pratt
- *Zapped*, Ann Louise Gittleman
- *Electromagnetic Radiation Survival Guide: Step by Step Solutions*, Jonathan Halpern, PhD
- *A Light in the Wilderness*, Catherine Thomas
- *The Kolob Theorem*, Lynn M. Hilton, PhD
- *A Brief History in Time*, Stephen Hawking
- *The God Particle*, Leon Lederman with Dick Teresi
- *Enoch the Prophet*, Hugh Nibley
- *Beginnings*, Carol Lynn Pearson
- *Everlasting Burnings*, M. Garfield Cook
- *Understanding Your Divine Nature*, Grant Von Harrison

Preface

If I need a defense for writing this book, it may be found in this quote by Arthur Schopenhauer: "First truth is ridiculed, and then accepted, and then it becomes set as an unquestionable fact."

I fear the facts in this book are true, but fear doesn't banish truth. Truth may prepare us to face the unsettling events of the coming tribulations. I feel certain technology will play a major role in the days prior to the Second Coming of Christ. We are entering those days.

Paradigm blindness is a condition in which we do not perceive things that exist outside of our currently accepted beliefs and experiences. But it is possible to experience a paradigm shift or perception change. Humans can expand their mental and spiritual context. We can then escape the confining mental structures of earthly language and thinking. At that point, we can receive new knowledge, new experiences, and a greater consciousness. When we ask God for knowledge, He will give us access to greater enlightenment. He can activate our spiritual eyes. We all have spiritual eyes, but they are not necessarily active. Our eternal spirits have an appetite for spiritual things. Our minds need to be spiritually engaged.

God promised He would pour out His Spirit on all people in the latter days or the end-times. If they are spiritually prepared, heavenly information and knowledge would be planted in the hearts of ordinary people provided they are susceptible to the whisperings of God's spirit and attune themselves to recognize the source of this precious direction. These souls are among us. We can learn to listen with our hearts and see with spiritual eyes.

> And it shall come to pass afterward, that I
> will pour out my spirit upon all flesh, and your

sons and your daughters shall prophesy, your old men shall dream dreams, your young men shall see visions and also upon the servants and upon the handmaids in those days will I pour out my spirit. (Joel 2:28–29)

J. Reuben Clark Jr., past apostle of the Church of Jesus Christ of Latter-day Saints, said: "God made it very clear that gaining spiritual knowledge is not a common place endeavor. He who invades the domain of this knowledge must approach as Moses came to the burning bush, he stands on holy ground, he would acquire sacred things; he seeks to own the attributes of deity, and the truths Christ declared will make us free. Sacred study removes all shackles of time and space."

Elizabeth Barrett Browning, Victorian poetess, described our situation very simply, "Every common bush is afire with God; but only he who sees removes shoes."

There is a rich spiritual formula around, above, and through all things. We call it the Light of Christ. Science calls it dark matter, although transparent matter or spiritual matter would be a more accurate name. Once we come to realize the power of this exquisite energy flowing through us, it maintains and influences our decision to either open our awareness more or block out entirely our spiritual awareness. It is a matter of personal attunement. My choice is to develop personal attunement. I am still at it. Perfecting this process is a lifetime endeavor.

There is a moving force of involved individuals feeling a powerful desire and interest in acquiring spiritual knowledge that will give them the Christlike depth and spiritual maturity to not only survive the end-time but also fully participate and accept the difficult days ahead. I call these individuals seekers. They instinctively feel that subtle sense of dread, unsettling vibes of some unknown earthly disturbance. An ominous feeling in the gut that something is wrong and out of sync. Both religious and nonreligious people are feeling on guard, waiting for the other shoe to drop.

Satan is abroad in the world and even the wicked who accept him recognize the increase of his great premillennial power. Along with the surge of evil, vile practices, and secret combinations in corrupt governments, there is also beginning to appear a promised millennial surge, a quiet celestial sun burst of pure revelation and core truths that when accepted will bring about an inevitable change in the individual. Knowledge is power. People are individually seeking spiritual knowledge that is coming in many forms.

A former apostle, Neal A. Maxwell, said it clearly, "For those who have eyes to see and ears to hear, it is clear the Father and the Son are giving away the secrets of the universe."

Answers hide right in front of our searching eyes. Seeing through spiritual eyes will clear away the fog. Pure revelation when accepted not only sets us apart in the world but also enables us to help the world.

There is a brotherhood of Elohim (gods) throughout a splendid and extended universe. Power emanates from all these in their dominions and flows in an unknown circuit back to them like a huge dynamo. Every good thought, intention, and action we as individuals perform glorifies our God and adds to His awesome reservoirs of power. It matters, you matter, and any righteous contribution is accounted for and accepted by God. Our goal is to become literally like Him. Therefore, our potential is to become at some point like our heavenly parents. They are gods and goddesses.

We know Christ attained equal glory and godhood with the Father, experiencing divine investiture of authority. Abraham, Isaac, and Jacob, as well as many other individuals, have all achieved godhood and received their own personal dominions. "Abraham received all things, whatsoever he received, by revelation and commandment, by my word, saith the Lord, and hath entered into his exaltation and sitteth upon his throne" (D&C 132:28–29).

As a young girl of ten or twelve, I overcame my hesitation and asked my Sunday school teacher a question. I cannot even remember the question, but the response of my teacher is still vivid. He pointed his finger at me and said, "Juanita, do not delve into the mysteries!" Coming from a less active home, I had no idea some things are classified mysteries. I realized I had crossed some invisible line. My teacher was perturbed, and I felt humiliated and embarrassed. It was many years before I dared to delve into the "mysteries of godliness." I wish my teacher had gently informed me these mysteries are to be sought out by each of us. We desperately need to move beyond the "lesser portion" of the word to the "greater portions" of the word, including the "mysteries." I have since learned these mysteries are not secret, they are sacred! They will be revealed as we are prepared by our Father to receive greater understanding.

Boyd K. Packer, formerly president of the Quorum of the Twelve, stated, "True doctrine, understood, changes attitudes and behavior. The study of the doctrines of the gospel will improve behavior quicker than a study of behavior will improve behavior. That is why we stress so forcefully the study of the doctrines of the gospel." God's promised endowments of knowledge and power requires that we must be both informed and transformed.

Earth life provides nonstop stimuli, vying for our attention and results in powerful distractions. As mortals, we also have to deal with internal noises such anger, desire, depression, sorrow, fear, self-will, illness, loneliness, and more. These are the characteristics of the natural man.

Earth is not our natural habitat. "God understands the burden it is to live with spiritual amnesia in regards to our divine home with Him in a preexistent state. He attempts to instill knowledge and faith to awaken us over time to our great potential." See book *Light in the Wilderness* by Catherine Thomas.

Just as some deny God, some in the world deny the existence of Satan. The denial is not only false, but also dangerous and is fostered by Satan himself. Satan is a personage of spirit as you and I and Christ were in the preexistence. In the premortal existence, he was a personage of great ability. Isaiah refers to him as a "son of the morning. "*How* art thou fallen from heaven, O Lucifer, son of the morning! How art thou cut down to the ground, which didst weaken the nations?" See Isaiah 14:12.

Satan cast from heaven still laments this banishment in his world of dark followers. Because of his all-out rebellion, the Father and Son could find no middle ground upon which they could mediate. Satan had to be cast out, not compromised with but cast out!

Jesus said in Matthew 6:24, "No man can serve two masters for either he will hate the one or love the other or he will hold to the one and despise the other. Ye cannot serve God and mammon!" Still, there are individuals who try to serve Satan without offending God. They play the middle ground but to no avail!

For six thousand years, a campaign for the souls of men has been waged by Satan with unabated fury. Suffering, sorrow, contention, idolatry, and wickedness sustained by the inhabitants of the earth testify to the fact that Satan has always wielded a potent influence.

Neal A. Maxwell provides perspective on what's coming. "Dangerous social movements are in motion. Science claims dominance and plagiarizes God's design. The world is looking for mass appeal instead of content. Everything to this point has been easy, but, get ready for a high adventure, men and nations finest hours come with the difficult times ahead. The most dangerous environment for us is when we live with so little light, that the surrounding darkness seems normal." He continues, "Don't seek out the storms of life. Be aware of the current news and subtle world movements, but filter them through the hope of the Gospel. Don't absorb the strife of our days, recognizing a day of sifting in the church and in the world is necessary."

All of us hit plateaus or flat stages in our spiritual journey. Some are tired and have fallen from their original enthusiasm in the church; some of us need to shut out the huge technological distractions. We need to refocus on the priorities that build our spiritual stamina.

"Satan's tactics, temptations, and soul-destroying strategies have not changed however, the unique challenge of the rising generation is that such tactics have increased in intensity and volume because Satan knows his time is limited." Yet a final warning from Elder Maxwell, "When you hear lukewarm Christians murmuring soft prophecies, such as all is well in Zion. Zion prospers! Remember, arrogance is a close relative to ignorance!"

Some of us think we know all there is to know about the Gospel of Christ. The basics will serve us well. What more knowledge is required? We know we are baptized members of the church. Is that enough?

"Sometimes some of us seem to indicate that having been baptized and periodically attending church services we are on the path to salvation. The elderly among us go into retirement, lean back and enjoy the thought, we have already contributed years of service, we will wait for our transport to heaven." President Hugh B. Brown then proceeds with this story, "This reminds me of a man who learned of a great discovery…Electricity!"

The man immediately had a conduit wire connected to his house, bought him a little 10-watt light bulb and installed it in the back room of his house. Then he sat down, put on his slippers, lit up his pipe, and sat in his rocking chair. He said, "I have electricity. No one can boast more than I because I have electricity too. He didn't realize that even with his little 10-watt light bulb, he was sitting in semidarkness. He had not understood that he could have had ten thousand times the illumination. He could have had a bulb in every room and over his piano, his front porch, and his reading lamp. But there he sits, placidly rocking, saying, thank God I have electricity."

He continues, "Sometimes, Latter-day Saints say, thank God I have the Gospel. I have joined the Church. I am going to heaven as soon as I die. There is an awful shock coming to some people, because the glory of God is intelligence. And there are some Latter-day Saints who have only a 10-watt light bulb of spiritual insight and knowledge. And that 10-watt light bulb will take them only where they use 10-watt bulbs. They won't be able to endure the glory of anything brighter."

Speaking of our individual learning obligation, President Brown states, "No person's lifetime is long enough to complete the lessons God has included in His glorious Gospel plan. Our spiritual education and instruction will continue into the next existence after we die. All we can take with us as we pass from mortality is our character and our knowledge. The wise Latter-d Day Saint will begin a rigorous spiritual head start program early in our lives that continues until we die, and then we will have barely scratched the surface of the knowledge God has to offer us."

Concluding his counsel in this area of teaching, he says, "It is critical as parents that we teach our children from infancy the Gospel of Christ. We have the golden eight, those eight years prior to baptism when Satan has no influence to tempt them. Set the standards, rules, and parameters that are crucial in place early. Clearly explain the expectations of our family, community, and, most of all, God's expectations as followers of Christ. If these guidelines are set early and reviewed consistently, they will grow and develop with the child, who is constantly observing your example" (President Hugh B. Brown).

When the Lord finally divides the wheat from the tares, it will be very plain to everyone what is about to happen. Those who have conscientiously served the Lord, performed missions, paid their tithes, kept their covenants, and kept themselves unspotted from the sins of the world will see the hand of the Lord revealed to rescue them from the terrors of destruction, which will begin sweeping across the earth. Those who only pretended to be saints will be remembered with abhorrence when it is finally revealed how much damage they did to the cause of Zion. Their fate will be sealed up with the rest of the wicked in the conflagration of destruction which will sweep the earth" (Cleon Skousen). This separation and sifting is a necessary part of the final judgment.

There will be unsettling events prior to Christ's Second Coming. They will enter with the burdensome spirit of deception. This deceit and trickery will be orchestrated by none other than Satan himself. He thinks he is forming a failsafe plan by bringing willing world communities into the "beast system." Satan initiated the war in heaven in an attempt to steal agency from all humans. He failed. Now this theft of our agency is being reactivated by Satan. Same attacker, different environment. Satan may use the technology tools available at this point in time to establish his modern governing plan.

People will surrender willingly by the millions in exchange for acceptance and inclusion into the coming technology utopia. It will be known as the New World Order and brings along its twin, the New World Religion. Modern science and technology seem to be partnering with this New World Order. People can choose to worship either or both. A government technocracy will be the centerpiece of government. All services will flow from technology. Every public need will be addressed through the beast centralized rule. The people of the world will be mentally and physically prepared to enter a world where all needs are met by the governing powers.

Satan will institute and establish the beast governmental system and cement the structures of control before most of us even notice his plan of entrapment. Satan cannot take our agency, so the awesome nature of modern technology and all it can offer humanity will be a personal choice. Who would not choose to join a new world order and all the benefits it will provide? We will lose agency by using our agency at this pivotal moment in history. There are times working at my computer when an offer pops up on my screen. The offer allows me to *accept or deny*. It is so simple. Push the accept button and you're in. Not only will you be included into the coming world order, you will be "frequencied" into the system, becoming part of the system. Push the *deny* button and you're immediately an outcast in society. The choice is simple if one is a follower of Christ. The only option is to opt out!

The leader of this final world government is the Antichrist. God's warnings are clear.

> And he (the Antichrist) causeth all, both small and great, rich and poor, free and bond, to receive a mark in their right hand, or in their foreheads: and that no man might buy or sell, save he that had the mark, or the name of the beast, or the number of his name. Here is wisdom. Let him that hath understanding count the number of the beast: for it is the number of a man; and his number is six hundred threescore and six. (Rev. 13:16–18)

When we love and serve God with all our heart, soul, and might, we are truly his children. His name is upon us, just as the name of our earthly fathers are upon us. We belong to God's family and carry his name. Take heart and have courage. God takes care of His own.

Acknowledgments

I need to acknowledge and give a shout-out of *thanks* to talented friends who entered and enriched my peripheral circle to assist my writing efforts. These special people and I were supported by a loving hand of God pointing to a worthy goal through a combined effort.

My husband, David Werrett

Writing a book changes the normal flow of life. My husband and family members were totally supportive and invested in my work. There were periods when the flow seemed to be a torrent, and they would throw out the loving lifelines and pull me to calmer waters. Many times they had more confidence and courage about reaching the goal than I. Thank you, dear family.

Anthony Patch

Anthony Patch is the most unrecognized and unheralded scientist in his field of expertise and perhaps even in the United States. He is an expert in the workings of the Large Hadron Collider at CERN, Switzerland, and an expert in the area of quantum computers and multi-facets of modern technology. He is also a student of the Bible and a dedicated Christian.

My awareness of Anthony Patch came as he guested on the Kev Baker platform centered in Scotland. I became immediately involved because of Patch's scholarly grasp of physics, his astute ability to transfer information, and a genuine candor and frankness about his subjects. He speaks with authority about science, and he speaks with humility about God. He has mastered the rich blend of science and religion, making it palatable for ordinary folks. He has a profound understanding of the effects and exponential power associated with quantum science and the technology revolution coming upon men. He has internalized very complex science theories, and then reestablishes this knowledge into a language that even I, a grandmother, can absorb and understand. He has a magical ability to manipulate complex issues into intelligible form. Thank you, Anthony Patch.

Vicki Plumb

One of my students offered to help me type my notes. She became very interested in the content. She prodded and insisted that the material be organized into a book. She pushed back against my resistance and response as to why I did not plan to take on such a huge writing effort. I told her I was too old and tired to embark on such a project. I explained to her, even with our combined energy, neither of us had the expertise to write and publish a book. I prayed for the right words to inform her of my final decision. I wanted to avoid her disappointment and help her accept my opposing decision. She would not accept no for an answer.

Thank you, dear Vickie, for your loving, determined, and occasionally irritating persuasion. Fortunately, neither of us had to accept "no" for an answer. True friends offer the necessary nudge.

Editor, David Tuttle

My husband and I attended the 2019 Firm Foundation EXPO held at West Layton, Utah. The expo featured classes relevant to the topics of our time. Many classes were offered during a three-day period. On the second day, I met a significant stranger who became an agent of change in my decision about writing a book.

On my way for a lunch break, I stopped to look at a book sale table. A man approached and asked if I wanted to buy a book. I had purchased all five of this author's books prior to his death. The man wanted to sell me a posthumous novel of this same talented author. I expressed that I didn't have time for novels right then because I was focused on scientific studies. He engaged me in a conversation about my current studies, and then took out his pen and he began writing notes. An hour later, we exchanged phone numbers and introduced ourselves. He then explained he was an editor, and he "birthed books." The book you are reading is the result of that meeting. My new found editor and friend passed away in the early stages of our work so I dedicate the finished book to David Tuttle. I am a believer in heavenly interventions rather than coincidental events. David and I realized immediately ours was not a random, coincidental meeting. Thank you, David Tuttle for believing in this project.

Lilly Occon

Lilly is a high school student and dear friend. She became my computer assistant and teacher. She is gifted at computer science and understands the ins and outs of Google Docs. She willingly accepted a summer job and became my skilled angelic computer "geek." That is an endearing term. She played a critical role in the computer mechanics and preparation of compiling a rough draft of this book. She was an invaluable asset. Thank you, Lilly.

Rudy and Hannelore Limpert

Thanks to the dynamic duo, Rudy and Hannelore Limpert. My dear lay-editors and neighbors, who were willing to be my sidekicks checking grammar and reading for story flow. Thank you for your support, time, and talent.

Introduction

The scripture, the prophets, and Christ Himself forewarned us of the great deceptions that would vex his children in this generation. Will you be deceived? Will I be among the deceived? Are we being deceived now?

I will attempt to alert you that we might all be deceived. I feel pressed to point out that any person on the path to find spiritual and scientific truth without acknowledging God and His Son Jesus Christ could ultimately be deceived through adopting counterfeit forms of science and religion. My definition of counterfeit is something made in imitation of something else with the intent to deceive.

Let's talk about basic scientific methodology. The scientific approach is as follows:

1. Observation.
2. Experimentation. Artificially producing what has been observed.
3. Theorizing. Seeking an explanation of the experimentation and original observation.

Science does not consider a fourth step. That step is *revelation*. Scientists negate and resist this sure method of seeking truth. However, we need this supplemental method to recognize things as they really are. The discovery of truth in science and religion requires careful and precise examination of the observable evidence, interlocking the temporal and the spiritual. True science and true religion dovetail as puzzle pieces complementing each other. Truth in every field gives peace and rationality to the soul.

There are priceless scientific principles disguising themselves in ancient and modern scriptures. These treasures are embedded in the Bible. See Genesis, Daniel, Revelation, and Job and also in ancient apocrypha and the modern-day translations of Latter-day Saint Standard Works of scripture.

Within scripture translated by the prophet Joseph Smith, true scientific pearls are embedded within his completed work titled *The Pearl of Great Price*. Abraham of old and the prophet of the restoration, Joseph Smith, were both inspired scientists in their own generations. They understood "greater portions of the word." They received the word directly from God.

Most Christians speed-read through the Bible. My advice is, "Slow down, partner!" A lot happens in the beginning. God created the earth and placed Adam and Eve in the garden. Adam was not deceived, but the woman being deceived was in transgression. Since both chose to partake of the forbidden fruit, a dramatic biological change took place in their bodies. The consequences led to the introduction of sin and mortal death. A new paradigm entered the cosmos. All creation would now be subject to these consequences. This initiated the critical need for a plan of redemption to save God's offspring.

Now the Great War in heaven had been moved to the garden by Satan, and he commenced a war between the seed of the woman and the followers of Satan.

The following is a quote from Sheri Dew that delineates this ongoing war: "There is no neutral ground in the universe, every square inch, every split second is claimed by God and counterclaimed by Satan!" Satan's goal is to destroy Christ and God's plans for us, then usurp the glory, honor, and power of both.

We know the end of the story, so does Satan, but his blind hatred toward man and his enmity toward God cannot be abated. Satan's constant raging hunger for power grows stronger as his time grows shorter.

And the great dragon was cast out, that
old serpent, called the Devil, and Satan, which

deceiveth the whole world: he was cast out into
the earth, and his angels were cast out with him…
Therefore rejoice *ye* heavens, and ye that dwell in
them. Woe to the inhibitors of the earth and of
the sea! For the devil is come down unto you,
having great wrath, because he knoweth that he
hath but a short time. (Rev. 12:9, 12)

Satan kicked his plan into high gear and enticed Cain to murder his brother Abel for material gain. This began the evil covenant of
occult practices with all the attending wickedness that then began to
contaminate the children of Adam. These preflood populations grew
hard in their hearts. They became past feeling and without natural
affection.

Fallen Angels, Giants, and the Tower of Babel

Now enters the strange teaching from Genesis 6, King James
Bible. It is a bit X-rated. It speaks of trusted sons (angels of God
having sexual interaction with human women resulting in corrupted
DNA that produced giants). Every wicked imagination of men was
acted out upon the earth. Humankind had willingly been contami-
nated by the spread of evil, and God was grieved that He ever created
man. The evil was so rampant that God decided to destroy all beings
and wash them away in a flood.

The Bible, along with many other ancient sources, clearly records
the existence of giants. David Wayne provides copious citations from
extensive apocryphal and Bible references, also numerous references
and historical material to bolster his contention. There are archaeo-
logical remains giving proof to the existence of giants. Remains of
their ancient skeletal frames are being discovered in archeological
digs throughout the world. What he uncovers will astonish you, and
it will challenge you to prepare for the fulfilling of God's prophecies.
These ancient bones were remains of the Nephilim.

When God cast Lucifer and his followers out of heaven, Lucifer set into motion a scheme to ensure the Nephilim (giants) survived. Why? Because from the bloodlines of these Nephilim some feel the Antichrist will come. To keep the plan alive, Satan has enlisted the loyalty of secret societies such as the Freemasons, the Templars, the Luciferians, and the Rosicrucian to conspire in teaching a theology and a history of the world that is contrary to the biblical one.

> This Genesis 6 conspiracy marches toward the Great Tribulation, when the loyalty of the Terminal Generation—this generation—will be tested. (*The Genesis Conspiracy* by David Wayne)

I know there were giants. I read about Goliath in the Bible. He had six brothers who lived in Gath in ancient Jerusalem during the time of King David. They were a genetic anomaly. They were fierce and threatening in their nature. They were also far more prevalent prior to the flood than we realize.

> And it came to pass after this, that there was again a battle with the Philistines at Gob: then Sibbecai the Hushathite slew Saph, which was one of the sons of the giant. And there was again a battle in Gob with the Philistines, where Elhanan the son of Jaare-oregim, a Bethlehemite, slew the brother of Goliath the Gittite, the staff of whose spear was like a weaver's beam. And there was yet a battle in Gath, where was a man of great stature, that had on every hand six fingers, and on every foot six toes, four and twenty in number; and he also was born to the giant. (2 Sam. 20:18–20)

Prior to 1887, most King James Bibles contained what was called the Apocrypha, i.e., the "missing books" of the Bible. Books such as Enoch 1, Jasher, and Jubilees, which provide incredible detail to the event that was/is alluded to in Genesis 6:2–3 (Septuagint version) snippets are also found in our King James Version of the Old Testament.

> And it came to pass when men began to be numerous upon the earth, and daughters were born to them, that the sons of God having seen the daughters of men that they were beautiful, took to themselves wives of all whom they chose. Now the giants were upon the earth in those days; and after that when the sons of God were wont to go in to the daughters of men, they bore children to them, those were the giants of old, men of renown. (Jude 6–8)

> The angels who took part in the unholy union with the human women ceased functioning as angels of God. Once this occurred, apparently they could no longer reside or even access Heaven and appear before God. These errant angels are referred to as fallen because the Bible said they left their first estate, in the heavens. In stark contrast, angels still abiding in Heaven never committed this horrific trespass against God's law. (David Wayne)

This view is further backed up by 2 Peter 2:4, "For if God spared not the angels that sinned, but cast them down to hell, and delivered them into chains of darkness, to be reserved unto judgement" (King James Version).

The fate of the fallen angels was incarceration by God who placed them into a designated holding space at the time of the flood. They lost their privilege of autonomy and the ability to roam and act freely. Their abode was a locked dimension or restricted environment controlled by God. The end-time scripture states they will be released once more, released into the environment of our earth. These entities will come as unwelcomed and unreformed troublemakers. Followers of the occult and secret societies hope for the restoration of ancient societies and the return of past rulers. Their hopes may have a chance of fulfillment in the new technologies of our day.

In contrast to what the fallen angels had engaged in, God stated, "Noah was a just man and perfect in his generations, and Noah walked with me" (Gen. 6:9). Noah and his descendants were only a few people in the world that were uncorrupted. In other words, the rest of the world was debased by sin and/or hybridization through the giants, men of renown, aka the Nephilim, DNA. However, Noah's bloodline, beginning with Adam from generation to generation, was untainted by corrupted angelic material. Scholars tell us that Satan's master plan was to eliminate the possibility of humanity's redemption by corrupting humanity's genome. More specifically, Satan's plan was to corrupt the bloodline of the Savior. Noah's bloodline, untainted by the Nephilim, was the critical bloodline emerging from the antediluvian world through which Jesus Christ would be born.

"Some of the hybrids found a way to survive, perhaps genetically through the flood. Regardless of how, there were giants after the flood, of which Nimrod 'became' one." Was there genetic manipulation or demonic possession involved in his transformation? We don't know. By Genesis 10 and 11, Nimrod had become a mighty one and had organized all of humanity into a one world government for "the whole earth was of one language and one speech" (*Revised Reality* by Anthony Patch).

According to the apocryphal book of Jasher, Nimrod had a three prong plan to conquer heaven and kill God. All these people and all the families divided themselves in three parts; the first said, "We will ascend into Heaven and fight against Him;" the second said, "We will ascend into Heaven and place our own gods there and serve them;" and the third part said, "We will ascend to heaven and strike Him with bows and spears." And God knew all their works and evil thoughts, and He saw the city and the tower they were building (Jasher 9:26).

Apparently, Nimrod had found a way to use the Tower of Babel as some sort of portal into heaven. He could actually see into heaven! According to Genesis 11:

> And they said, go to, let us build us a city and a tower, whose top may reach unto heaven; and let us make us a name, lest we be scattered abroad upon the face of the whole earth. And the Lord came down to see the city and the tower, which the children of men builded. And the Lord said, Behold, the people are one, and they have all one language; and this they begin to do: and now nothing will be restrained from them, which they have imagined to do. Go to, let us go down, and there confound their language, that they may not understand one another's speech. (Gen. 11:4–7)

Their languages were changed, and they could no longer have an understanding useful enough to complete the building projects.

The unbelievable may become believable as we march forward into an unusual future of science, genetic innovation, and technology. Now, as in Nimrod's day, God may have to halt our progress. Maybe we too are at the point where men have advanced their science so far into God's domain that a restraint is required.

Jesus stated He would return in a day when society would again resemble Sodom and Gomorrah and circumstances would be "as in the days of Noah." The technocratic elite and the high priests of science in our day could be repeating the history of Noah's time. The parallels are shocking.

Satan's strategy is universal and timeless. His devious plots can work in any generation. He merely restructures the same plan to fit a new situational opportunity that could provide him power. Satan is not dealing with the spiritual amnesia we suffered as we acquired mortal bodies. He remembers and kept appreciable intelligence allowed him in the preexistence.

Our modern technology increases Satan's options for inroads to disturb and entrap man. His goal is to separate us from God and destroy the promise of personal salvation. We must not underestimate the workings of the enemy. He hates God, and we being in the image of God are included in that same hatred. Satan declared war against God in the beginning. His war has not ended. There is a spiritual fight coming from the throne of Satan himself. It is time to suit up, show up, and stand up for Christ. From the days of Cain and Satan's alliance, a written log of dark arts, occult practices, blood oaths, hidden knowledge, and secret combinations became available to those who sought them out.

Those seeking unmerited wealth, power, and complete control of others are in full engagement of these powers; they are steering their final programs. Secret societies and dark combinations involving global control of all nations are in coordination with the coming technology revolution. The technology is now in place to mark, surveil, and manipulate every person on the earth and coerce cooperation in exchange for survival in the new tech age.

Advertising and marketing the public has always proved useful to persuade buying. In our world of technology and public dependence on electronic devices, purchases are possible 24-7. In fact, the most radical change in world history has evolved through something called "productive programming" in mass media. Productive programming appears in movies, television, computers, cell phones, and emails. It is a form of brainwashing. Marketers realizing populations exposed to this soft brainwashing stimuli will bring about "behavior modeling responses" in large groups of people. Product sales are appreciably increased with a consistent nudging of shoppers.

This know that in the last days perilous times shall come. (2 Tim. 3:1)

For then shall be great tribulation, such as was not since the beginning of the world to this time, no, nor ever shall be. (Matt. 12:21)

As you move into the beginning chapters of this book, it will become clear that we have been coddled concerning science since grade school. The science and technology manipulation continues today by academics locked into a scientific orthodoxy they can ill afford to have overturned. Why? The public is easier to deal with if they are "dumbed down" and preprogrammed to believe we are incapable and uninterested in their field.

Center for Human Technology co-founder, Tristen Harris presented these thoughts on *CBS This Morning News* on October 2019.

It seems as we are upgrading technology, while we are downgrading humans:

We are shortening the attention spans of humans.

We are seeing a rise in youth mental issues: self-harm, depression and suicide.

We are increasing human addiction to their devices.

We are increasing social isolation in people.

We are rewarding outrage and cultural misconduct.

We are polarizing politics.

Part of the technology business model is the extraction of the human attention system in a race to the bottom of the brainstem. The tech companies are too big and too powerful. They are sacrificing security for clicks.

We must reevaluate what we were taught in science class. Don't let science frighten or deter you. We also need to search out the new revelations and precious knowledge overlooked in the area of religion. Information is helpful, and accurate information is powerful. In our present situation, ignorance is not an option!

America came through the agricultural revolution; we entered the industrial and information revolutions. Each of these events stretched and challenged the cultural norms of world populations. The adjustments to these jarring calibrations were intense! However, nothing in the history of the world will change the social paradigms or rattle the comfort zones of millions like the appearance of the new quantum computer technologies and world 5G telecommunication systems that are quietly in play right now. These powerful systems will blanket the earth and integrate all humankind. These technologies will change the standard technology paradigms forever. Listed below are a few currently developing technologies that will alter human existence:

- Self-driving vehicles
- New forms of packaging and delivery
- Virtual assistants
- Neural external and internal components placed in and on our bodies
- Brain interfaces
- Space travel rockets
- Humanlike robots
- Cure for cancer
- Crisper DNA editing and reverse aging
- Transhuman augmentation
- Decoding of human brain operations

In addition, the populations of the world will be introduced to many other technology miracles we have not even dreamed of. These advances will surely change the cultures, morals, and behaviors of individuals worldwide.

Overview of Super Technology Tools

Our culture is being programmed to accept full incorporation into the world of high tech. The following technology systems will support and merge with the 5G telecommunication networks. These following technology structures are in place now:

- Blockchain is the operations platform

- 5G is the telecommunications system
- SWS is the surveillance system
- Quantum computers will serve as the inter-dimensional system
- IoT. Internet of things is the all-inclusive coverage system
- AI. Artificial intelligence is programmed machine intelligence duplicating human intelligence.

Augmented and virtual reality, smart devices, and robotics represent the unimaginable-related technology in beginning stages. I will give you an overview of some remarkable systems that are being riveted onto our societies worldwide.

The *blockchain system* was first introduced through the arrival of Bitcoin cryptocurrency. It depends on human greed to absorb us willingly into the digitized currency system. To visualize this system, think of actual blocks called "nodes" hooked or chained together. Each one of those blocks or nodes represents a person, as you and I. As more people participate, more data is collected on the individual blocks. Massive amounts of data is being added 24-7. The blockchain system is the data collection structure. The recent explosion of Bitcoin triggered governments and businesses to look at the possibility of digitized currency for all. Many have introduced new digitized coin under different names. Each company could realistically have their own coins, like Amazon coin, Walmart coin, or Google coin. These could emerge to the end that brings about world government control of all currency, perhaps Fedcoin.

The blockchain system has all the components necessary for the beast system architecture to build end-time government. World citizens will have been properly prepared to become compliant participants in the established order. Blockchain will become so pervasive that it will take over our lives. It will require our personal data in every area of our daily activity.

The *5G system* is a fifth generation telecommunication system. The FCC will now open even higher frequency bands for the new powerful 5G system powered at sixty gigahertz. This is a military band wave developed for weaponry frequencies. In 1996, Bill

Clinton passed the Telecom Act. This law allows federal, state, and local governments the freedom to proceed unchecked with the powerful telecommunications we are faced with today. Systems so technical and complex, citizens cannot understand them. Communicating tools that upgrade and change so fast they become obsolete as soon as we pay for them. Our older cell phones today are powered at 4G levels. At some point, a huge upgrade on all personal devices will be required for all users as we enter the 5G construct.

The 5G is all about one thing—sending massive amounts of data across the internet at incredibly fast speeds. And while this concept might seem basic, you are about to see there is nothing basic about 5G technology. The 5G will bring us not only smartphones, but also smart appliances, smart houses, smart cities, and smart nations. CNBC had this to say about 5G, "The tech economy depends on it, without it the technology revolution would stop." No one is speaking about the dangers of high frequency radio waves on humans.

Smart devices. Smart homes and smart cities are coming. My state of Utah has agreed for Salt Lake City to join New York as the first two cities to become smart city testbeds (see *Deseret News*, Kelly Hill, April 10, 2018). Salt Lake City will be totally run by 5G, including autonomous cars. The upgrade is in process. Cell towers along with relay units will be located every eight hundred feet to afford necessary transmission coverage. Other states are vying for the privilege and money it will generate.

Salt Lake City is also poised to build a unique inland port in the downtown industrial area of the city. It will be a national hub for transporting goods coast to coast. Major trucking and high speed rail will support this expansive endeavor. This will connect in with the "smart city construct."

Sentient World Simulation System. In 2006, Purdue University initiated this new surveillance mechanism. It went live in the United States in 2007. This is a self-awareness system that calculates psychological prediction of human behaviors. It can set up situations and study human behavior and reaction to planned events in real time. This is a massive psychological testing and experimentation system that is running continually. It has been progressing and improving for some time. Digital copies of our information feed into the SWS. Data and behavior patterns of humans become predictable and can be anticipated through the use of artificial intelligence.

This system will present testing to observe the reaction of mass populations, individuals, and groups. Programmers have set up scenarios to record public reaction to specific events and circumstances manufactured in the general populations. The study can predict human behavior and their responses to stimuli through carefully planned social events.

We are participating in a huge experiment without our knowledge. Mass populations are being observed. Predictive behavior patterns emerge. In the huge technology industry, we are the product, and our data is the new gold. The Sentient World Simulation program is a fully developed surveillance system that is becoming nationalized around the earth. There will be a full incorporation of all populations. The surveillance powers and control of the ruling class will be so heavily weighted on the side of government that citizens will basically become modern-day slaves.

The *Internet of Things* (IoT) is an all-inclusive system where all things are captured on the internet. It is also called "edge" computing because there are no edges that are not covered. All "input and output" is accounted for. Nothing remains outside the system. All books, papers, documents, currencies, personal data, and government records, *everything* is included in the system. This system depends on 5G.

This is a breakthrough technology that enables physical devices to "talk" to each other and operate with increased efficiency, making everything from smart cars to smart appliances, to smart cities and grids, possible.

I personally attempted to purchase new Whirlpool double ovens, and they no longer make anything but "smart ovens. I returned it and ordered a different brand. That choice will soon be impossible, because "smart meters" will be mandatory here, as they are in California (see stop the crime.com, Deborah Tavares).

With all the advantages and awesome results that come through these systems, they could and might be used for nefarious and population-damaging outcomes. The danger of exposure to increased radio waves on humans is a critical issue that needs to be addressed.

Robotics efforts are not new. Patents go back to 1989. Artificial intelligence and robotics have been discussed over a period of time. Scientists foresee the impact and are making strong efforts to harness the great power through placing AI in robots. AI has brought in a new age.

Science claims this progress is a celebration for individuals. We will be benefactors of more freedom, more convenience, and more joy in the technology utopia. Really? We will be offered avatars and robots that are identically fashioned in our likeness. These will be so exacting they can prove as legal identification entities.

Elon Musk stated, "The population will not know the inherent dangers of robots living among us until they witness robots killing people on the sidewalk." That seems a bit extreme to me, but do we really understand the powerful combination of AI placement in robots?

Quantum computers are the paradigm shift in the complex world of computers. The quantum computer, AI relationship is a worrisome issue because of the awesome adaptability. It is a symbiotic relationship that increases the power of both.

D-Wave Inc. is the world leader in manufacturing quantum computers. Geordie Rose is the main spokesman at D-Wave Systems located in Burnaby; British Columbia. This enterprise excels over US companies in this new quantum computer field. These computers are giant metal black boxes ten feet by twelve feet that are refrigerated on the inside to temperatures of one degree of absolute zero. These are the coldest temperatures engineered and a hundred times colder than interstellar space.

At the heart of the box is a complex armature hooked to the top hanging down four to six feet long. At the very bottom of the armature is a tiny chip the size of your thumbnail. There are hundreds of quantum qubits on a chip. On this chip is all the wonder and magic that makes startling things happen.

See black box image.

See armature image.

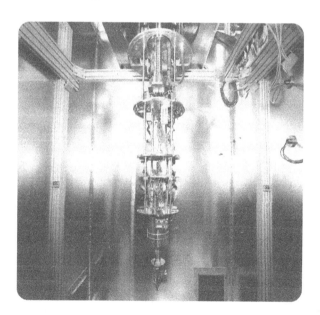

The *Boltzmann machine* is a deep learning system. The Boltzmann machine brings about a new paradigm. This instrument of communication no longer remains unconscious, dormant, or insentient. It is a support system and a fully engaged partner to artificial intelligence. This AI titan uses recursive neural networks and connections between all units to form a directed cycle learning system. It uses unsegmented things like handwriting recognition or speech recognition. These abilities set it apart from the forward neural network settings. The new D-Wave computers in connection with the Boltzmann machine, AI technology, and the Blockchain system are the remarkable combination for an unbelievable paradigm shift in quantum computing and interconnected telecommunications systems. These will all work in tandem.

The Boltzmann machine can gather all data resources at the geometric levels at increased speed in real time. It can tunnel through peaks and valleys on a flat plane, tunneling at the lowest gravity state. This state holds all the answers. This technology can search all problems and reach all solutions within highly decreased time periods.

Augmented and virtual realities.

"What comes after smartphones?" (Jeff Brown, *Casey Daily Dispatch*, November 12, 2018).

Our cell phones will become obsolete. The technology replacement will be AR, "augmented reality." There will come a day when you can work from the comfort of your own home and simply "teleport" via hologram to the office to chat with colleagues or sit in on meetings. With the use of an AR headset, desired graphics, images and data are overlaid on top of the world you normally see. In twelve to eighteen months, these AR wearable devices will look more like fashionable trendy eyeglasses.

AR technology is still an early prototype, but eventually you will be able to text, call, check emails, and browse the web by using voice command, hand gestures, and eye movements while wearing intuitive AR glasses. All information will appear as if it were floating just a few feet in front of your face. The 5G is revolutionary and will be incorporated into wearable AR devices. The impossible will become possible.

Digitized DNA (deoxyribonucleic acid) is the instruction manual for all living organisms. It is a massive storage system. A single cell is the size of a small period. Our owner's manual is encoded in our personal DNA. It can replicate itself and is self-correcting. Enzymes make repairs as they move up and down the genetic helix.

Something has changed in our day. We are in the early stages of a powerful technology that has hit the scientific world by storm. The change is life altering. This revolutionary technology is called CRISPR (clustered regularly interspersed short palindromic repeats). It will be a curse or a great blessing in the near future. The CRISPR system is a miraculous gene editing tool that is precise, cheap, and relatively easy. It is almost like a DNA surgeon. The technology could cure or bring the end of diseases, solve the aging process, and possibly postpone death. It could also modify the whole gene pool of humanity. Modified humans could become the new standard. Whatever your opinion, this modified future is here. What has been insane scientific fiction is about to become our new reality, full of opportunities and challenges.

DNA lasts for hundreds or even thousands of years if kept at moderate temperatures. Could this be why Egyptian burial practices were so focused on almost a compulsive preservation of the dead bodies of their royalty? Were they planning for a restoration and return of these honored ones?

Were Satan and the embalmers of Egypt hoping for a time far in the future when digitized spiritual entities will be set free, a day when science provides plasma conduits that form interstellar bridges over time and space? Could these conduits provide passage of pollutions of unknown origin? We are not sure what could take advantage of an open tear in the fabric of space. There could be transference of bacteria, viruses, spirit entities, undiscovered DNA, a flood of data, and foreign energies. Great volumes of transmitted data could pass through these conduits within nanoseconds.

The followers of Satan might have anticipated a golden era when science would develop interdimensional connections that bridge time and space. Could the ancient ones (demons and fallen angels) come forth to take up position for the great end time battles?

Each of the foregoing new technology discoveries is teetering on a delicate horizon. Man has stretched science and his complex brain to new heights. These outcomes are dangerous beyond our wildest dreams. They can also fulfill our most awesome dreams for the benefit of men and the world.

A virtual AI enhanced, 5G world is on our doorstep. Will it be a friend or foe? This technology can be a perilous burden or a remarkable heaven-sent blessing. It is truly a two-edged sword.

We are facing a science, technology tsunami. How do we handle a tsunami? To be candid, I don't know. We may be caught up in it, we may drown in it, and we may bob around in it until we get our sea legs. Some of us will come to accept and welcome it. Others will recoil and reject the life-altering technology offerings.

A lot depends on whether we can trust the "technology gods" who will control it. I am feeling less and less comfortable that they have our best interests in mind. Money, power, and control of the masses have a powerful appeal to those in charge.

I would like this book to give my readers hope and excitement in the possibility of positive outcomes. Current events and future circumstances may lead that direction.

As an observant grandmother feeling the determined hand of age on my shoulder, I realize my time here is limited. My children and grandchildren will face the full impact of the future. I have a potent hope combined with heavy concerns for the coming generation. They are the technology generation. I trust them, and I trust in God. This does not mean that for numerous sleepless nights, the facts of my study did not materialize into a frightening scenario that haunts me still. As I connect all the technology dots, they form a very unsettling web.

The Antichrist Triumvirate

I see the system of the beast. A system that is almost impossible to opt out of. Satan tried to abrogate our agency once before. He lost that battle!

Are we prepared for a New World Order? Let's envision the final predicted New World Order or the governing system of the beast found in Bible scripture.

There are two dominating personalities that appear in the end-time scenario. They will impose the Antichrist system and culture prophesied as the Last Days found in Bible scripture. We are in the final dispensation of the earth prior to the Second Coming of Christ. He will then usher in His thousand-year millennial reign of peace. Before this blessed existence arrives, we will go through some very, narrow daunting, and deadly straits.

Prior to that time, Satan will wield great power, and he is preparing two wicked men waiting in the wings. They are both deceitful, hypocritical characters. According to scripture, these will lead a final world government for a designated period of horror. One is the Antichrist and the other is the False Prophet.

The Antichrist is a political man who acts like a religious man, and the False Prophet is a religious man who acts like a political agent. They are both duplicitous.

The actual Antichrist figure will position himself as God. He will put in place a Middle East Peace Plan that will be honored and sustained for three and a half years. He will be an orator who is speaking great words. He will also be cunning, charismatic, cruel, and a popular cultic figure. He will head up the governing arm of the system.

Second in position is the False Prophet, who controls the ecclesiastical or religious arm of the system. He supports the convincing half-truths and empty promises of the Antichrist leader. This devious prophet is the false religious shepherd of the New World Order religion.

In Revelation 13, we read

> And there was given unto him (the antichrist) a mouth speaking great things and blasphemies; and power was given unto him to continue forty and two months. And he opened his mouth in blasphemy against God to blaspheme His name and His tabernacle, and them that dwell in it. And it was given unto him to make

> war with the saints; and to overcome them; and
> power was given him over all kindred and tongues
> and nations. And all that dwell upon the earth
> shall worship him, whose names are not written
> in the book of life of the Lamb, slain from the
> foundation of the world. (Rev. 13:5–8)

Both of these figures are under the control and influence of the archenemy, Satan. You will recognize the structure of an unholy, counterfeit "triumvirate," Satan, the Antichrist and the False Prophet. These three impose global rules.

This False Prophet will mandate worldwide worship of the Antichrist and introduce an economic system that requires full allegiance through the "sign of the beast." When one accepts the sign of the beast, one is also allowed participation to buy or sell. There will be no merchandising outside of this system. Those Christians and outcasts who refuse to worship this imposter will be reduced to barter for survival and can expect to become martyrs of the modern age.

The Time of Jacob's Trouble

There will be a final seven-year period prophesied in scripture prior to the Second Coming of Christ. These final seven years complete the seven-year tribulation period known as the time of Jacob's trouble. Jacob refers to the Jews. Keep your eye on Israel.

Three and a half years into this seven-year period, these two demonic Antichrist tyrants will lead the world onto the horrific stage of Armageddon. The war to end all wars will rage for another three and a half years. The second three-and-a-half-year block marks the finish of the final seven years. Christ will step in near the end of the seven-year tribulation to stop the conflict or there would be no flesh left.

> And except those days should be shortened,
> there should no flesh be saved: but for the elect's
> sake those days shall be shortened. (Matt. 24:22)

This arrival of Christ is the Second Coming. Hallelujah! This is His return. Bible reading of Daniel and Revelation will give you more detailed information associated with "end-time" prophecies and warnings.

Sherri Dew comments, "Critical mass comes into play when corrupt political systems, secret societies and gangs become so prevalent that the helpless smaller resistors are threatened, harassed, and often murdered. When God's sword of justice falls on the wicked, its reach will also fall on the ignorant, the deniers, the complacent, the appeasers, and the cowardly, all those who refuse to stand against evil!"

False religion and secretive science have become bed partners. Nightmares could ensue.

Apocalypstein is the Greek root word meaning "to uncover, reveal or disclose." We are instructed in the Book of Revelation that all things will be restored, and there will be a restitution and return of all things coming into one great whole, a heavenly disclosure. We are at this time recognizing greater levels in religious and scientific advancements. We will understand the merging properties of particle science and God's science with clarity. God is uncovering His mysteries regarding the unique pairing of spirit matter and temporal matter. God's true scientific theories will be understood by all.

When Jesus Christ comes, He will expand knowledge in all fields beyond our wildest dreams. The Father and His son, Jesus Christ, are the source of all scientific and spiritual laws in the universe. They are quantum mechanics and particle physics originators and masters.

The earth will undergo significant structural changes and be restored to a former state. In this tumult of revelation and disclosure, God promised all truth will be revealed. The end-time environment may usher in the final uncovering and restitution presenting itself in areas of our current science and technology.

I am a woman of God, and I realize fear and faith are not compatible. I am choosing faith; my faith rests in God the Father and His Son, Jesus Christ. They are fully aware of the end-time events. They are allowing them but will orchestrate the coming judgments to their fulfillment.

Prophets, from the time of Adam, were shown signs and events leading to our very day. These prophets were instructed to write scripture containing clues for those who will live through the culminating events. God has assigned prophets through the ages to sound the warning cries for our day. They plead for us to follow God. Most people in the world are choosing the gods of technology over the true God. The predicted signs are appearing for those who will see. I am praying my book will at least provide a small admonition that can be heard above the noise of the technology stampede. The overall progression of the momentous tribulation adventure is in process. I am putting my life and future in the hands of God. He is the ultimate technology master.

PART 1

Can We Reconcile Science and Religion?

Chapter 1

High Priests of Science

It is critical in this day of discovery and augmented scientific knowledge we come to an accurate balance of understanding between foundational science and foundational religion. They are not incompatible. In fact, for the safety, peace, and comfort of humanity and the earth, we need to learn and rely on the truths and laws embedded in both areas.

Having studied the direction of science and technology over these past years, a quote by Omar Bradly, chairman of the US Joint Chief of Staff 1948, resonated with me.

> Our knowledge of science has clearly outstripped our capacity to control it. We have men of science but too few men of God. We have grasped the mystery of the atom and rejected the Sermon on the Mount. Man is stumbling blindly through a spiritual darkness while toying with the precarious secrets of life and death. The world has achieved brilliance without wisdom, power without conscience; ours is a world of nuclear giants and ethical infants.

This chapter will help us examine a comparative between God's scientific arrangement and the scientific methodology of man.

Scientists, agnostics, and atheists claim the universe came about without intelligent impetus or creative source. The laws of the universe developed without guidance or directions. It simply occurred by time and chance.

Nonplants crossed the great chasm to become plants and non-animals to become animals and invertebrates to vertebrates. Without guidance or cause, primordial ooze developed a brain where none had existed and sensory organs where nothing like them had ever been. Randomness accounts for the delicate unique composition of the earth, this oasis of life in the vastness of a hostile universe.

The skeptics believe man is without a spirit, and his existence ends at death. Man's existence is an accident, his work is fruitless, and relationships are ultimately meaningless. Man's mortality is instilled by "organic evolution." They purport there is no master plan for mankind. For some scientists, evolution is a more convenient theory.

N. Webster: Evolution is "a manifestation of related events or ideas in an orderly *succession*, as in a process of growth... This theory, according to which the *higher forms* of animal life are derived from the lower...holds that *all* animals and plants are descendants of a very few simple organisms (or perhaps of but one)..."

W. Weaver said, "The great Darwinian movement has seemed to many to constitute a major indication that man, if he is indeed nothing but an improved beast, can by one more easy step be nothing more than a machine—and thus surely an object in which science can wholly analyze, wholly capture within its special framework" (Am Sci, Mar. 1961. "Evolution: A Convenient Fiction," January 1, 1900, by Ben Crowder; Charles Darwin, creation(s), creationism, Darwinism, evolutionary theory, guesswork, higher forms, prehistoric man, probabilities, speculation, systematic theology, teleology, theories. G-2 report, number 3).

Scoffers and nonbelievers ignore the biblical record. The singularity of the Bible is just an incredible coincidence. Forty diverse men writing over 1500 years kept separate records and historic events, which independently foretold a remarkably similar story. The challenge facing the skeptics is, their judgment of God is rendered according to their limited understanding.

Scoffers have a limited view, which can be compared to the position of a flea living on the back of a large dog, issuing a solemn evaluation that because he can't see the whole of him, there is no dog. Clearly, the flea is not only foolish but also totally wrong. The dog is everywhere. Whether the dog really exists is not dependent on the flea's perception.

The book of Job is a science chronicle. He was a desert dweller in the Middle East. His book is probably the oldest written scripture ever. His writings are believed to have predated the book of Genesis. Who instructed Job in science, astronomy, climate, structure, and earth cycles? Who schooled him about physics, nature, and universe phenomenon? Did he have access to scholars, scientists, ancient libraries, or educational centers? Who taught him? Yet scripture written by Isaiah, Job, and Abraham also explains modern-day science in detail.

Science explains away scientific knowledge found in the scriptures and deep understanding of the universe given to men tutored by the creator Himself. Modern scientists have reduced all scientific findings to equations, charts, and graphics. The one thing science cannot provide is what the future holds for man. There are too many variables for accurate prediction. They have ignored the spiritual laws inherent in scientific endeavors. They refuse to calculate in the art of prophecy. They refuse to recognize God developed not only spiritual law but scientific law also.

There are, however, some scientists willing to recognize another view. Freeman Dyson,_"The more I examine the universe and the details of architecture, the more evidence I find that the universe in some sense must have known we were coming."

Robert Jastrow comments, "The essential element in the astronomical and biblical accounts of Genesis is the same chain of events. They both reveal man commenced suddenly and sharply at a definite moment in time, in a flash of light and energy." He also states, "For the scientists who have lived by faith in the power of reason, the story ends like a bad dream. He has scaled the mountains of ignorance; he is about to conquer the highest peak; as he pulls himself over the final rock, he is greeted by a band of theologians who have been sitting there for centuries."

We must have faith that true religion and accurate science are always reconcilable. We have the witness of many Latter-day Saint Church leaders in regard to such a belief. John A. Widtsoe stated in the preface of one of his books, "This volume is based on the conviction that there is no real difference between science and religion. The great, fundamental laws of the Universe are foundation stones in religion as well as in science."

Ezra Taft Benson was equally straightforward in a 1966 General Conference: "There can never be a conflict between revealed religion and scientific fact. Spiritual truths cannot conflict with the truths uncovered by scientific endeavors."

My study of quantum physics has shed new found enlightenment and a startling revamping of understanding for me. I found the scriptures, especially the end time scriptures, even more impressive.

Daniel the prophet could not understand what he saw in his vision of our day. It was so troubling to him that he became ill and took to his couch for weeks. He was told to seal up the book. Only the people who live in the end time would recognize through the spirit the unusual signs. God promised that in our day, new writings, records, and events would be unsealed and presented. "But thou Daniel, shut up the words, and seal the book, even to the time of the end: many shall run to and fro, and knowledge shall be increased… And he said go thy way Daniel: for the words are closed up and sealed till the time of the end" (Dan. 12:4, 9).

I have sympathy and love for Daniel, the prophet who took to his bed and exited his post in the palace of King Nebuchadnezzar, for weeks after he saw the events of our day in a vision. He saw improbable, outlandish technology that terrified him. You and I may be unaware witnesses who could actually be living, surrounded by the scenes Daniel experienced in vision. Like Daniel, there may be days we take to our beds in fear. However, like Daniel, I know the great God Elohim is the source of all power, and He manages the laws of the cosmos. This plan is His. We are in His hands. However, as I study the end-time prophecies, I feel science and technology may be allowed to hasten fulfillment of God's dire prophetic warnings.

I am asking you to get your spiritual eyes and ears accustomed to an outpouring of "end-time warnings" and unique biblical messages. We are the people of the end-time. We are the ones privileged to see the extraordinary days heralding the millennium.

Edison vs. Tesla

Scientists have divided themselves into two camps. There was a tug of war between Nikola Tesla, Thomas Edison, and the United States government. Tesla had a superior theory. He hoped to draw energy from the atmosphere to provide the power needs of the country. Tapping into the atmospheric resource would be free for all people. It would be a natural energy source available to the world.

Tesla needed government support for research and financial backing to implement his project. He invented the Tesla coil, which proved battery power placed at the bottom of the Tesla coil automatically increased as the power moved up the coil. Energy levels revealed a natural power surge increase with upward movement. The Tesla coil was a basis for his theory that AC electric power was present everywhere in unlimited quantities and could possibly drive the world's power grid and generate free electricity to all populations

With the advent of his discovery of the light bulb, Thomas Edison felt certain he had the new technology for the future. He approached the government with a profit making plan. Instituting a patchwork plan of poles and stringing electrical lines across the country would begin an electric grid system providing jobs and establish a permanent billing charge for people requesting power to their homes. Wealthy promoters concurred. Edison's theory won the day. He and the government destroyed Tesla and left him a beaten, washed-up figure in the dustbin of history. Tesla was treated with humiliating disregard, but his theories were more correct than anyone admitted or allowed.

Science is finding there is a high energy, mysterious, invisible matter filling all of space. Currently, scientists are secretly and selectively using Tesla's basic electric universe theories. Why? Because it works! Tesla understood a universe filled with powerful electromagnetic "plasma," an all-inclusive, unending, invisible, power source of light and energy found in, though, and around all things. His theories are expanding. Most programs and experiments are relatively unnoticed, and some are disguised in the most public of places. One place is the Large Hadron Collider at CERN near Geneva, Switzerland.

Switzerland is similar to the Vatican; it has a legal and political governing structure that allows scientists to work in a protective environment and provides a clandestine atmosphere. The Swiss government operates under a secretive independent statehood system with their own police force. The Swiss practice a neutral stance as to neighboring countries. Banking transactions are subject to zero transparency. One reason for the Swiss border location of CERN is because the Swiss authorities exempted CERN from all regulatory safety inspections concerning experiments and testing at the collider. This release from encumbering safety rules is unusual.

The Large Hadron Collider

Let's get acquainted with CERN and the European Organization of Nuclear Research. ES5 is the European open science cloud working as a fiber optic network connected to CERN. There are 160 laboratories with synchrotron linear accelerators created in the US alone. These associated scientists are deeply interested in following the experiments occurring at the CERN location.

The collider at CERN was a joint effort supported and hailed by international scientists from around the world. The stated goal was to smash particles down to the original building blocks of the universe. Science was on a search for the first primordial building block of the universe. They sought the "god particle."

In our day, the World Wide Web brought together scientists of all backgrounds and languages to build and participate in the world's largest particle accelerator at CERN. The languages of international scientists were translated and easily understood through computer programming. CERN is suggested to be the temple of modern physics. It is also called the Second Tower of Babel.

The very structure of the ancient ziggurat spiral towers had power inherent in their structural form as do hadron colliders of today. The spiral towers mimicked Tesla's coil, producing increasing power with upward and circular movement. The preflood ancients had appreciable technology skills and scientific ability. The armature of the new D-Wave quantum computer has similarities to the same specific architectures.

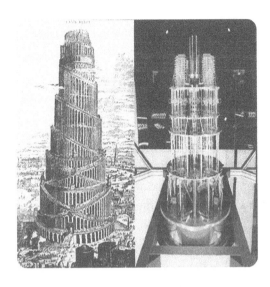

The ancient tower of Babel was brought to an abrupt halt. God changed the languages among men to stop the goals of Nimrod to reach through portals into heaven. His plan was to make war on God. (See image Pieter Bruegel, famous painter.)

The Large Hadron Collider is the largest man-made machine ever built. Building commenced in 1957. The aboveground building is dome-shaped architecture.

It sits on the Swiss-French border, near Geneva, Switzerland.

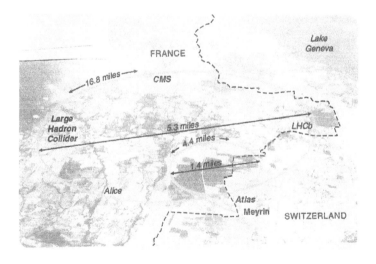

It is centered in the little village of Pouilly. This word in French means "Apollyon or Apollo."

The LHC itself is positioned at the powerful electromagnetic nexus of ley lines atop the ancient site of a temple built to worship the sun god, Apollo. To this day, the villagers claim they live above the abyss or pit prophesied in scripture. "And he opened the bottomless pit; and there arose a smoke out of the abyss as smoke of a great furnace" (Rev. 9:2).

The actual collider main ring is three hundred feet underground, nestled beneath the ground level building and forms a seventeen-mile doughnut-shaped tunnel. It is kept at cryogenic (outer space) temperatures. This is where the powerful colliding of subatomic particles takes place. Let's peek into the massive collider machine and observe the process.

The high-powered circular speeds of particles inside the accelerator produce enormous energy levels. Most of the Large Hadron Collider ring is made of incredibly powerful magnets, which steer the beams in a curved direction following the ring because the protons must be forced to travel in a circle. The nature of these particles is to travel in straight lines plowing through all obstacles.

The LHC magnets number some 1,232 in total, each being 16.6 meters long. Their total weight is forty thousand tons. Accelerating the protons inside the pipe cavities located in the tunnel increases their energy and keeps them in tight bunches. These pipes inside the tunnels work at a chilly -268.7 degrees and are bathed in liquid helium to keep them cool. Operating at such low temperatures, these superconductors carry huge electric currents.

Proton particles are fed into the tunnel system at high and increasingly higher speed. The strong magnets surrounding the tunnel impose heavy compression forces that squeeze the particles into two tight compacted beam forms. The tremendous force of two high energy particle beams racing in opposite directions at nearly the speed of light three hundred feet under your village is a bit unsettling.

In June of 2008, a German, chemist, Otto Rössler (University of Tübingen) attempted to bring a lawsuit against CERN in the European Union Court of Human Rights. His lawsuit could not prove "credible threat." The courts tossed the suit out, but this court case succeeded in generating heated discussion of a possible dark side to the experimentation at CERN. (Anthony Patch)

In September 19, 2008, at the CERN complex, there was an accident, and in less than a minute, forty million dollars in damages occurred with no one even aware until after the fact. A shoulder joint in the pipe leaked and caused a pressure wave in the tunnel. The force of the wave through the tunnel surprisingly activated the emergency shutdown unit. A horrendous crisis was averted without human casualties.

If a loose power beam is no longer going through the directed path and escapes, it plows through concrete and surrounding earth with great destruction. There are two small villages set 330 feet above the ring on the Swiss-French border.

Public welfare doesn't seem to be the major consideration. With governments and technology leaders in control, the protected experiments at CERN seem to come first. There is a top echelon of scientists, participating governments, technology titans, and wealthy interested insiders hoping for positions in future global planning. Technology will likely be the foundation of the new world government structure.

However, there are thousands of dedicated scientists and others who are simply practicing their field of interest with a genuine desire to participate and contribute. Personal discovery is their sole motive. Many universities fall in this category. They are fulfilling grant requests and following specific directions to accomplish the results, they are commissioned to produce.

If a scientist disagrees with sponsors, he can be penalized, often severely. The rule is "publish or perish," which means going where the funding is and staying away from controversy. "Leaving it to the scientists" is not always a good idea. There are still a few "mad" scientists.

The force of escaping beams would bore a hole more than a quarter mile long through any material. Going upward, it would extend hundreds of feet above the village in the air. The damage would be immeasurable. So, keeping the beams controlled is crucial. Colliding the beams inside the tunnel have been compared with firing two knitting needles from opposite sides of the Atlantic Ocean and having them meet halfway.

At a predetermined point, the circulating beams are programmed to cross, causing a quantum level collision and powerful subatomic explosions. These explosions generate billions of particles at once. At that point, the detectors start taking precise measurements of critical data in real time. It is like sifting every grain of sand on a beach at once and keeping track of each grain.

CERN has thousands of computer operators around the world collecting computer data; even private people do "data mining for them."

The collider runs a few months out of the year, and there are regular shutdown periods for major cleaning and repairs. It takes months to prepare for experiments, and additional months to bring the collider ring up to speed. The huge magnets placed around the collider ring have to be warmed up in preparation for the beam runs and gradually cooled down after testing. CERN science is secretive. The scientists engage in minimal public reporting of test results at the facility. The internet is a good source for information on CERN, and the collider testing schedules can be accessed at CERN injector Schedule.com.

The Higgs Boson

Past and current explosions have resulted in the discovery of at least one thousand new particles. Among them is the claimed God particle now known as the Higgs Boson. In July of 2012, CERN announced the discovery of the primordial God particle. It was named the Higgs Boson after scientist Peter Higgs. We will compare this unique discovery to the true God particle shortly.

The worthy study and expertise of our modern scientists who have made such remarkable findings in the area of particle physics is noteworthy. The discovery of the Higgs Boson warranted accolades and world recognition is due. This discovery gave rise to the theory of the Higgs Field, which proposes an invisible energy field throughout the universe. Scientists are now coming to understand this totally pervasive energy. They call it dark matter, antimatter, invisible matter or the Higgs Field.

Tesla named it plasma. It is invisible. It only reveals itself by the pull it exerts on the galaxies. The long held gravity theory has been adjusted because science has found the attracting power is not great enough to credit it as the sole cohesive function.

All things from galaxies down to atoms must be held together by some more powerful function. It is part of the primary creation and sustaining force of existence within our reality. The rotation speeds of galaxies would tear apart if not for some form of nonvisible matter holding them together. We will learn about nonvisible matter.

The Higgs Boson (God particle) does exactly what the Bible says God does. He holds the universe together at the molecular level. Jesus Christ, using powers bestowed on Him by His Father, created the heavens and the earth, the visible and invisible. The Greek root word for hold together is *sunistemi*, meaning "compacted, or cohere together."

This cohesive God force is at work in our bodies. We all have a laminin protein as the binding property that holds us together at the cellular level. It glues our cells together, then to a foundation or scaffold of connective tissue. This keeps every cell in place and working properly. The laminin protein is shaped like a Roman cross. Is there a deep theological significance in the shape of these critical proteins? Yes! You bet! One cannot believe in an omniscient God and such an unintended coincidence.

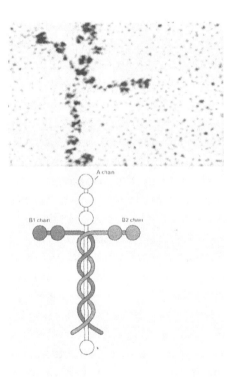

Look at a simple module of the nucleus of an atom. It has positive charged and neutral particles. The natural electrostatic repulsion between the positive protons would naturally drive the nucleus apart if not for that strong force, which holds the nucleus together. There is an active force imposed on the universe that actively holds the very atoms of visible matter together from moment to moment, day to day, and century to century.

Intelligent properties of spiritual matter requisitioned and instructed and controlled by God and Christ through loyalty and cooperation of the intelligent components of spirit matter serve this purpose. There is no way to account for this phenomenon apart from an active, omnipotent, all-wise God.

Imagine what would happen if every atom in the universe were allowed to come apart. Peter had a vision of just such an event. "But the day of the Lord will come like a thief in the night; in which the heavens will pass away with a roar and the elements will be destroyed with intense heat and the earth and its works will be burned up" (2 Pet. 3:10). Coherence? For how long? As long as God determines!

"Numerous high energy experiments over the years have occurred in the synchrotron collider deep underground at the CERN facility. Scientists were searching for the primordial building blocks of the universe. The interest was in finding this elusive quantum particle of matter and the glue that holds it all together.

"The scientists at CERN, their sponsors, and government are pursuing forces that are the glue of life through which we exist. They are finding forces that create and forces that annihilate. These scientific barbarians have no idea what they are smashing. The pursuit of ultimate knowledge and ultimate power to control the destinies and future of everything, including humanity, always ends in ruin!" (unknown quote).

At CERN, atoms are blasted down into components that are never meant to be split apart and blasted into isolated particles. These function as a whole atomic ecosystem. How do they function as separate entities? Are they doomed? Are we doomed? The goal at CERN is to strip away the boson, the binding material (primal glue) and discover the original building block of the universe.

Prior to his death, Stephen Hawking expressed concern because the Higgs Boson is very unstable. He feared CERN testing could cause issues like mini black holes or generate a cataclysmic vacuum decay causing space and time to collapse. We would have zero warning, as we, the earth and possibly the universe, is winked out of existence.

Astrophysicist Neil de Grasse Tyson warned the experiments at CERN could literally cause the planet to explode.

A telling quote by Neil de Grasse Tyson gave me pause for thought. "These high priests of science and assisting monks in private computer sanctuaries dotting the world have our lives in their hands. Why are we not completely outraged by this 'ticking time bomb' called CERN? CERN and all related ventures should be shut down and dismantled completely and immediately!"

Following the CERN explosions, blasted particles leave this natural matter unbalanced, unattached, unnourished, and separated. These are not meant to be separated. At the Large Hadron Collider, scientists smash blast and separate. They destroy life to discover the building blocks of life. You cannot learn about life by pulling it apart. You cannot know about life by destroying it. What you may learn about is death! We need to recognize the special value, awe, and beauty provided by an unaltered natural universe. It is something to be cherished.

We have a living universe that is being explored and exploited. Some see space as the new frontier where perhaps resources and land could be acquired. National governments and industry see profits, control, and power positions in outer space.

Word is circulating that scientists at CERN are delving into inter-dimensional realms as well as running a suspected space weapons program secretly. They are exploring kinetic and directional weapons that render nukes to firecrackers. CERN could be developing into a secret space weapons developer hence a plan for a new

"Space Force" addition to the US military. (A recent direction from Donald Trump, President of the US):

> Pres. Trump set in motion the new branch of the military, the US Space Force on December 20, 2019, as an operational arm of the military with a two-hundred-man organization. Establishing an additional funded military structure will require considerable new funding. It will definitely grow from this small beginning." The first graduating class of NASA space rangers is called the Artemis Graduates. This excited group of military space rangers is aiming for travel to the moon and from there to Mars within the next five years. Three new rockets with unique features and modern design will provide travel back and forth to the space station where these astronaut students will study and train for now. We will no longer be dependent on Russia for transportation. Commercial flights are in the near future. Virgin Galactic is a commercial company planning to fly citizens into outer space. They have seven hundred customers willing to pay a $250,000 fee for this unusual travel opportunity. Their timetable is within the next five years. (United States Space Force, *Fox News*, Bill Hemmer Program, 1/17/2020)

Is Science a Religion?

Science has become a religion. It is a non-Christian religion. The high priests of science are obedient to their own facts and theories. They are working with God-created particles, experiments, and outcomes. They handle, manipulate, and even crash and smash particles with zero acknowledgment of God, the creator, Himself.

CERN scientists have reached their primary goal. The Higgs Boson has been found; now they can shut down this questionable enterprise, right? No! The scientific and technology goal posts have moved, and CERN is evolving.

Scientists left God out of the equation, but they are now embarking upon His mysteries without Him. In the rush for power, they have abandoned restraint. It seems to me that men of science and technology are probing into God's domain, and we may all reap the whirlwind.

> Thou art wearied in the multitude of thy counsels. Let now the astrologers, the stargazers, the monthly prognosticators, stand up, and save them from these things that shall come upon thee. Behold, they shall be as stubble; the fire shall burn them; they shall not deliver themselves from the power of the flame; there shall not be a coal to warm at, not fire to sit before it. (Isa. 47:13–14)

In addition to the Higgs Boson, a new mysterious particle was discovered. These mysterious particles show up when collider speeds exceed ten TeVs (tera electron volts). These particles are thrown off as debris. These new particles are nicknamed "strangelets." They are super stable particles and cannot be controlled. As soon as they hit the north field, they sink directly to the center of our earth.

In addition to the CERN collider, there are over a hundred smaller synchrotron colliders in the US that are testing at speeds higher than ten TeVs, and no one knows the rate of increase in strangelets from this combined testing. Numerous accelerators can run beams higher than ten TeVs, which produce "quark gluon condensate" (strangelets).

The debris field at CERN is an area in the middle of the accelerator ring and is called the north field. All collision remains and debris is steered into this dumping area. When you factor the multiples of quadrillions of particle collisions directed into the north field area at

CERN, the powers are astronomical. The collisions are breaking the bonding properties of subatomic particles using super force levels. These amounts of energy if harnessed could possibly push through into other dimensions. They may open galactic portals in deep space or travel to areas of inner earth dimensions. This sounds like science fiction turning to science truth. However, these possibilities are not lost on the scientists at CERN.

What Are Strangelets?

Strangelets are intensely belligerent, unruly little particles. They have minds of their own. They cannot be captured or controlled. They are so magnetically dense they sink immediately to the magnetized core of our earth. There they keep collecting with subsequent tests. Strangelets are the most explosive elements in the entire universe. They are composed of three quarks—an up quark, a down quark, and the strange quark, (hence the name strangelet) held together by gluons. This particle is also called quark gluon condensate. I call this God's super glue!

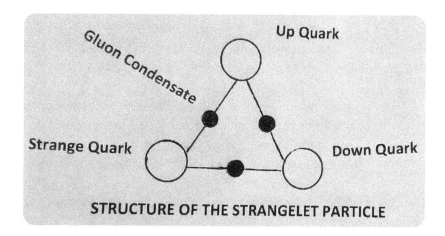

STRUCTURE OF THE STRANGELET PARTICLE

Strangelets have mass and inter-dimensional traits. They have the potential of becoming superpowered galactic weapons. This rogue particle is the perfect power source for opening the quantum micro dimensions in the tiny subatomic environment and macro dimensions in distant outer space. This particle product could become a horrific weapons component.

They have tremendous magnetic power fields, many times the magnetic field of the earth. They have a powerful influence on all surrounding matter. They draw magnetized matter forcefully toward their core. So how do we deal with strangelets? No one knows, not even the nine thousand international scientists associated with CERN. They offer shallow reassurance of public safety, then push forward future planned experiments.

These newly discovered particles are not discussed openly because of the dangers involved. Would academics and citizens object to the production of strangelets? Yes! That is why these results are denied and kept in the dark. Knowing the dangers, we would all object and reject such experiments.

Could these collecting strangelets be pulling surrounding matter to themselves, increasing a hyper density state at the core of our earth? Yes! This is the very process that changes planets into brown stars. Brown stars forcefully draw surrounding magnetized matter into their center until the star suffers death through implosion. Granted this could take thousands of years. However, there is growing proof something is affecting the true magnetic north pole readings. Earth's magnetic north pole has shifted away from Canada and closer to Siberia at a rapid pace in recent years.

- Researchers believe two massive blobs of molten iron in earth's outer core may have spurred the runaway pole.
- There's no telling where it will end up.
- The movement has been so rapid that the British Geological Survey and US National Geophysical Data Center, which update the World's Magnetic Model, had to accelerate their process in order to keep up.
- These shifts have major consequences for global navigation systems. Anything or anyone that uses a compass—

from ships at sea to the smart phones in our pockets—is impacted by this magnetic game of tug-o-war.

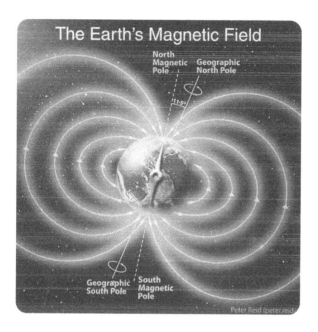

The magnetosphere is the natural shield protecting us from the ionized radiation directed at earth from the sun. Might these growing levels of magnetism be affecting the natural shield surrounding our earth? This bizarre particle could also become a horrific weapons component in the wrong hands. This is all new untried physics. Scientists have no idea of the result, but they doggedly continue experiments, seldom considering the unintended consequences.

When testing the atom bomb, there was an unexpected side effect not factored in by scientists. As the bomb exploded, it sucked in great amounts of the surrounding atmospheric element, and the expected explosion was shockingly greater than anticipated. Unanticipated consequences happen often in science and technology. Scientist, Robert Oppenheimer, early director of the Los Alamos Labs, following the first atomic bomb explosion on July 16, 1945, shared a famous quote from the Bhagavad Gita, "Now I have become death, the destroyer of worlds."

There are some concerned scientists who are sounding the alarm bells about the work going on at CERN, but they are quickly silenced. Scientists and the modern tech titans have ignored God, silenced concerned fellow scientists, and kept unaware world citizens in the dark.

Chapter 2

Compare the Present with Noah's Era: The Two Enochs

In the preflood era, there were two important men who are worth mentioning. They were both called by the name Enoch. One was righteous before God, and the other was wicked. Both Enochs were in possession of hidden powerful knowledge originating from God. Now we must recognize the "wicked" Enoch, who was a direct descendant of Adam and Eve through their son Cain (Cain conspired with Satan to murder his brother, Abel). Cain, his son Enoch, and their descendants manipulated and distorted this rich fuller knowledge of angels to push forward the dark goal of Satan and his followers from the beginning.

The ancient "science of the craft" is the dark arts from the days of Adam originating through Satan. Numerous apocryphal writings have surfaced, revealing a fuller picture of the unique Pre-flood prophet, Enoch. Those magicians and sorcerers seeking power and hidden knowledge through divination allows communication with the entities (fallen angels) that release Enochian math and language. This foundational knowledge may have slipped into modern-day science and technology through a small circle of believers of divination and modern-day necromancy. The diviners and necromancers of Noah's time brought the flood through their decadent practices. The modern high priests of science, through similar practices, could be the very ones who bring about the final prophecy of destruction through fire.

We will recognize the righteous Enoch, a descendant of Adam and Eve's son Seth.

"And Jared lived one hundred and sixty-two years, and begat Enoch; and Jared lived after he begat Enoch eight hundred years, and begat sons and daughters. And Jared taught Enoch in all the ways of God" (Moses 6:21 Pof GP). Through his righteousness, he and his whole city of Zion was translated by God and taken into heaven, sparing them from the horrors of the future flood.

The following are titles of ancient texts referring to righteous Enoch. These were discovered in more recent times.

- The Hebrew Book of Enoch
- The Syriac Apocalypse of Paul
- The Slavonic Secrets of Enoch
- Ethiopian Enoch
- Laurence's Enoch
- The Greek Enoch
- The *Dead Sea Scrolls* (Book of Enoch) found in the Qumran Cave #4, Aramaic fragment
- "Enoch's writings are 'theodicy,' the vindication of God's justice is a clear component of Enoch literature" (Hugh Nibley)

Enoch had many names that describe his character traits and spiritual power: Enoch, Henock, Enosh, the weeping angel, the teacher of righteousness, the great initiatory, the teacher of heaven, the heavenly scribe, man of intelligence, the venerable scribe, and the conveyor of cosmic knowledge. He had priesthood power over the elements and ability to establish a Zion City of God.

We get a revealing overview of preflood times in the *Collected Works of Dr. Hugh Nibleys, Volume 2: Enoch the Prophet.*

Enoch was the great preflood prophet who established the City of Zion. Enoch is relative to our times. His was a wicked world on a collision course with disaster. He lived in a world devoted to dark pleasures and men who were resolute and sophisticated in their waywardness. Peculiar to the world of Enoch was not only the arrogant quality of the sinning that went on, but also the high degree of enlightenment enjoyed by the sinners, making them singularly culpable before God. They had used their agency to reject God. Through their spiritual apostasy, they stubbornly continued their ruinous course, ignoring God's commandments and blaming others for their misfortunes.

The technology of Enoch's world was introduced by purveyors of secret, hidden knowledge that was spread among them. They practiced advanced technology and sciences. Even their children were acquainted with the arts and mysteries. The dangers and unintended consequences of their abilities were known, but they felt they could outsmart nature and God. They were learned in chemistry, metals and weapon construction, manufacture of dyes, jewelry and cosmetic formulas, drugs, astrology, and incantations associated with the dark arts.

The goal was to emancipate them from any dependence on God through technological know-how. This may sound foolish, but they knew enough science, technology, and the ruling principles that governed the cosmos, so having this knowledge, they felt no need for God. The great danger to all existence was that the perverters knew too much. They had learned the secrets of angels and practiced the violence of Satan. The threat was from those who had received the ordinances but removed themselves from the law of the gospel. They had set up a counterfeit religion as a way of life.

Theirs was not mere naughty behavior, it was a clever inversion of values that could never be set right; it could only get worse. This was a clear contradiction of what God intended. It was a clever imitation of the "true order of things. Corrupt practices were being riveted permanently onto the social order."

Enoch tells of the physical and moral pollution of the earth. Only a great purging and cleansing of the wickedness infecting the earth could rectify the decline. God has agents He uses to purge. They are water, fire, and wind. Without such a periodic cleansing, the world would not be able to endure the sins of mankind.

Enoch experienced hearing the earth's painful cry for relief found in the *Pearl of Great Price* scripture. "Woe, woe is me, the mother of men. When shall I rest, and be cleansed from the filthiness which is gone forth out of men" (Moses 7:48).

Wickedness proceeded until at length, God corrected it. He returned the earth to its primal state. He covered the earth with water as it was in the beginning. He allowed the global immersion of the earth.

> For as the lightning, that lighteneth out of the one part under heaven, shineth unto the other part under heaven; so shall also the Son of man be in his day. But first he must suffer many things, and be rejected of this generation. And as it was in the days of Noe (Noah), so shall it be also in the days of the Son of man. They did eat, they drank, they married wives, they were given in marriage, until the day that Noe (Noah) entered into the ark, and the flood came, and destroyed them all. (Luke 17:24–27)

Why did so many drown in the flood? The same reason so many will be burned when Christ comes in judgment the second time. God will need a cleansed earth environment. The filth and wickedness is so burdensome for the earth and vexing to the righteous it will require an intense overpowering burning to enact final judgment. This end-time conflagration lies ahead of us. The ancient prophets saw our day and testified of the actual event.

As in the days of Noah, blatant wickedness of men brought stern judgment from God and is a reminder to us that both flood and fire destroy errant men. At the same time, ridding the earth of corruption through the pervasive flood could have blessed our earth with a holy preparation, a baptism by immersion, preparing the earth for its future sanctification. The second holy ordinance for the earth will be baptism of *fire*!

Preflood men had totally rejected the seeds of salvation God's prophets tried to plant. Men used their agency to choose evil. That choice triggered the violent reactions of the earth, pushed back the light and spirit of God, and men felt the wrath and destruction that ensued.

God is required to limit gross sin through destruction of these increasing wicked behaviors. Man's power for evil was almost unlimited, so God allowed a cosmic shift in the normal workings of the world. Those who were destroyed would have destroyed everything.

Enoch asked the Lord, why are there destructions? And the Lord answered without hesitation, "Behold they are without affection!"

> I gave them knowledge, I gave them agency, and I gave them two great commandments. I asked them to love one another and commanded they should have me as their Father. (Hugh Nibley from his apocryphal writings of the *Book of Enoch*)

Judgments Pronounced upon Our Day

Isaiah admonished us with this instruction:

> Come my people, enter thou into thy chambers, and shut thy doors about thee: hide thyself as it were little moment, until the indignation be over passed. For behold, the Lord cometh out of his place to punish the inhabitants of the earth for their iniquity; the earth also shall disclose her blood, and shall no more cover her slain. (Isa. 26:20–21)

This final judgment will dispense with the wicked and prepare a paradise for the righteous. Fire is a purifying agent. The cleansing will be thorough! Most citizens of the world will be totally unaware of this cataclysmic event until it is upon them.

Prior to this final event, disbelievers and the wicked will mock God and the prophets. The days of tribulation will cause shock and awe. Worldwide religious and nonreligious masses will be awaiting a totally different finale. The three great religions are awaiting the arrival of three separate saviors or Messiahs. Christians are awaiting Christ, The Muslims are waiting for the "twelfth imam," and Jews anticipate the unknown messiah who saves them from total destruction in the final great war called Armageddon.

Followers of the occult hope for the restoration of ancient societies and for the return of occult gods and goddesses to resume the golden age. The occult practices are reappearing and are quite open and spreading throughout modern world populations currently.

Being a devout Christian, I prefer to adhere to the Bible and restored scripture returned to us through Joseph Smith, the prophet of the final dispensation. The scriptures are filled with valuable information concerning the critical events of our day. There are specific signs and holy warnings presented. There will come a great revealing and warning through prophets who speak the words of God.

> How oft have I called upon you by the mouth of my servants, and by the ministering of angels, and by mine own voice, and by the voice of thunderings, and by the voice of lightnings, and by the voice of tempests, and by the voice of the earthquakes, and great hailstorms, and by the voice of famines and pestilences of every kind, and by the great sound of a trump, and by the voice of judgement and by the voice of mercy all the day long and by the voice of glory and honor and riches of eternal life, and would have saved you with an everlasting salvation, but ye would not! Behold the day has come when the wrath of mine indignation is full. Behold verily I say unto

you, that these are the words of the Lord your
God. (D&C 43:25–27)

The future coming of the apocalypse may require the opening
of a sealed portal covering the abyss. A key will be required. Students
of the end-time have puzzled over the "key," but until our day, the
thought of an encryption key or code was never considered. The
opening of dimensions, portals, or wormholes may be accomplished
through the use of coded frequencies or encryption keys.

And the fifth angel sounded, and I saw a
star fall from heaven unto the earth: and to him
was given the key of the bottomless pit. And
he opened the bottomless pit; and there arose a
smoke out of the pit, as the smoke of a great furnace; and the sun and the air were darkened by
reason of the smoke of the pit… And they had
a king over them, which is the angel of the bottomless pit, whose name in the Hebrew tongue is
Abaddon, but in the Greek tongue hath his name
Apollyon. (Rev. 9:1–2, 11)

This angel who holds the key opens the pit that releases darkness, wickedness, hell, burnings, and locustlike creatures. This angel
was a king with authority. He is clearly named in more than one
language. Abaddon and Apollyon are both names referring to Satan.

Portals, Wormholes, and Parallel Dimensions

Many believe there are strategic places on earth, which are portals, gates, stairways, and entries to other dimensions. These openings
could be passages leading into or outward from the earth. Science
speaks of wormholes and parallel dimensions in space.

For those who read the scriptures and believe them to be the
Word of God through His prophets realize openings and coverings

in space sound familiar. In the Holy Scriptures, God tells us of His stretched-out curtains and veils that separate earth from heaven.

"Prepare for the revelation which is to come, when the veil of the covering of my temple, in my tabernacle, which hideth the earth, shall be taken off, and all flesh shall see me together" (D&C 101:23).

It is very possible that God compartmentalizes His space and assigns dimensions and areas for His massive creations. There are many heavens and hells and degrees of both depending on the inhabitants.

The pope of the Catholic Church took the Apache Nation to court to get control for the construction of the Graham Mountain Deep Space Observatory. The lawsuit brought to light the reason Native Americans fought the building of this observatory on this particular mount. Both, the Catholic Church and the Native Americans, felt this was a holy mountain. Indians feel it is a spiritual "portal" into the heavenly environs of God.

Of course, the Catholic Church won and is the proud owner of the largest deep space telescope in the United States located on Graham Mountain, Arizona.

> Mountains were God's first temples. They have significance to the Lord. They should be significant to us. We need more men that can match the mountains. We need to be mountain top men. Moses went to Mount Sinai to commune with the Lord, he ascended Mount Nebo to view the promised land. The Lord commanded the prophet Isaiah with these words, "Get thee up into a high mountain." Christ preached the Sermon on the Mount. It was a high mountain where Christ was transfigured before Peter, James and John. Jesus loved the Mount of Olives overlooking the temple and the holy city. (Sterling W. Sill, *Leadership Volume 2*)

For Native American Indians, Graham Mountain designated a spiritual entry point to their god. It was a holy high place to commune and interact with deity. The negative lawsuit outcome was a bitter pill for the Indian community.

Are these modern pipe dreams of entering parallel dimensions or portals merely science fiction illusions? Is this even possible? As a skeptical questioning grandmother, this interaction of inter-dimensional contact in any form stretches belief. However, disbelief can be overcome by fact.

I will share some facts associated with the Birkeland Current phenomenon.

Definition: Birkeland currents are a set of currents that flow along geomagnetic field lines connecting the Earth's magnetosphere to the Earth's high altitude ionosphere. The strength of the Birkeland current changes with the activity in the magnetosphere.

The Birkeland currents were discovered in 1908 by Norwegian explorer and physicist Kristian Birkeland who undertook expeditions to the Norwegian Polar region to study and shed light on the aurora borealis phenomenon. Hannes Alfven, a Swedish engineer and plasma physicist, promoted Kristian Birkeland's ideas and put them on paper in 1939. We know today that these remarkable currents exist. This set of currents flows along geomagnetic field lines in the magnetosphere, high above the Earth's ionosphere.

Birkeland Currents

The Birkeland currents are twisting, spiraling charged plasma-like magnetic ropes. These can form twisted helical shapes called flux ropes or flux transfer events (FTEs). Birkeland currents form scalable plasma structures that can transmit electric power throughout the galaxy. Electricity moves along Birkeland current filaments that bind the Sun to its family of planetary bodies. Birkeland currents almost always occur in pairs and often spiral and twist around each other like a double helix. These are supersonic plasma sets. The twisted pairs create a field aligned current flow that follows the magnetic field in space. These volatile currents allow electric power to travel vast distances.

CERN and D-Wave are tinkering with the possibility of changing the spin of quantum particles to produce movement and emanations riding on the electrical magnetic ropes of the Birkeland current to reach other dimensions. These currents could emanate massless energy to carry information through a vacuum at one billion times the speed of light. Energies lacking mass are things like digitized DNA, spirit entities, knowledge or thought transfer. These emanating transfers seem abstract, but they are perceptible properties originating from a source.

Once established, this conduit might have permanency, and all things taken down to their molecular level could transport back and forth through this helix-shaped electrical conduit. It seems poking into other realms may be possible.

The Bible speaks of angels who were allowed to come to earth, entering in through specific portals to teach men hidden knowledge in areas of deep science, working metals, alchemy, and technology. These angels were punished by God and lost the possibility of returning back into heaven. They forfeited their first estate because they succumbed to sexual interaction with the beautiful daughters of men.

"For if God spared not the angels that sinned, but cast them down to hell, and delivered them into chains of darkness, to be reserved unto judgment" (2 Pet. 2:4). The fallen angels were locked up prior to the flood. Scripture states they will be released once more.

Scientists at the Large Hadron Accelerator in connection with the new D-Wave quantum computer claim they now have established inter-dimensional properties. Have they opened portals or torn the fabric of space to observe forbidden realms? It is concerning to me that CERN has some obvious connections to the occult practices. The acronym CERN comes from the Roman god of the underworld, Cernuous or Hermes. He is the god of the underworld. This seems an unusual moniker.

The spirit of our age seems to honor the occult. In front of the CERN building, there is a large statue of the Hindu poly-god, Shiva. She is the goddess of destruction and ruler of the dark. The CERN logo is a stylized 666 emblem. In scripture, this numeric symbol identifies the Antichrist prophesied to come in the end-time. One visiting the Large Hadron Collider will see this emblem prominently displayed on the grounds.

Here is wisdom. Let him that hath understanding count the number of the beast; for it is the number of a man; and his number is six hundred threescore and six. (Rev. 13:18)

Sergio Bertolucci, director general for research at CERN 2017, stated, "The LHC could open a doorway to an extra dimension. Out of this door might come something, or we might send something through, opening a portal or conduit into another dimension is the goal." Many feel this quote by the past director holds a more sinister objective at the CERN facility.

The word that forms *technology* comes from the Greek root (techi) meaning the "art of the craft" and refers to wizardry, witchcraft, stargazers, fortune-tellers, the alchemists, and magicians. These were the keepers of hidden knowledge. The hidden mathematics and language known to God were usurped and corrupted anciently by the fallen angels. They were accepted and used by fallen men.

I fear that a few of our modern scientists today may have tapped into questionable resources and reestablished connections to the occult, thereby gaining access to hidden knowledge through summoning willing tutors and schoolmasters from the "dark side."

I realize how crazy these things sound, but my concerns are not based on flimsy myths and rumors. My foundational studies and understanding of the new computer and technology strides occurring right now in the world are grounded in solid fact. The troubling outcome reveals the origins of our new science and technology challenges our Christian religious foundations. False religion and secretive science are dangerous bed partners, and both are sharing the nocturnal dreams of a worldwide technocracy trap.

In the next chapter, we will meet the new quantum D-Wave computer developed in British Columbia. It is an inter-dimensional computer that is sending seismic waves through the computer technology world. The developers of this new computer claim to have actually delved into an alternate dimension. Geordie Rose, the CEO of D-Wave, states his claims of a superior intelligent race that will soon appear. He stands next to his new D-Wave computer. It is a large black refrigerator cube encasing armature supporting the miraculous quantum chip system.

This computer is tuned to the background frequency of the earth and has an audible beat every few seconds. Rose states, "The steady heartbeat tone of his machine has a deep effect on him." I feel like I am standing at the altar of an alien God? The key word here is "alien." Maybe the connection is with darker entities in Satan's domain?

The quantum chip system is much more than even the creators at D-Wave have realized. The Higgs (God) particle is part quanta temporal matter married to intelligent spiritual matter glued together by a boson called light. (the photon). This marriage was made in heaven through God's fine-tuned plan of "duality." Science has entered God's domain uninvited.

The relatively new D-Wave company has close connections with the CERN facility. They partner on numerous experiments. CERN using a newly discovered strangelet particle, which would have the necessary power to open an inter-dimensional portal. A quantum computer would be the ultimate tool required to control the size and closing of such a manmade opening. There is great danger of an uncontrolled process. There could be a danger to humankind and the earth itself.

New Agers talk of our being in the fifth age—the Age of Aquarius. Their belief is a new evolving Utopian future and culture of great intelligence, a time of visitation from our ancient star ancestors or an alien culture. The Bible tells a different story; it tells of a spiritual battle, a continuation of the war fought in the preexistence in heaven. In his wicked determination, Satan's war continues and intensifies against the people of the true God and His Son, Jesus Christ.

The warning is precise and clear. Ours will be a spiritual battle, and the beast system will nearly overcome the saints and almost dampen the faith of the elect.

"For we wrestle not against flesh and blood, but against principalities, against powers, against the rulers of the darkness of this world, against spiritual wickedness in high places" (Eph. 12:6). The science of today excludes God and may be delving into dark science and—I may add—dangerous science.

> The greatest enemy of knowledge is not ignorance: it is the illusion of knowledge. Today ignorance is not an option. (Anthony Patch)

A great technology delusion is in the making. We are being programmed like experimental mice. It includes mind control and dependence upon our technology that will be all consuming. The awesome advantage and usefulness of computers will not only be increasing and appealing but almost worshipped. It brings to mind a jarring quote by historian, John Wheeler Bennet, regarding the rise of the Democratic Socialist Nazi party, in Germany: "Not until they riveted the fetters upon their own wrists, did they realize who indeed was captive and who was captor."

The world population will demand full participation. The new science of technology and false religion will merge and the touted unity will come in the form of "hive mind" manipulation when people willingly allow external control of their thoughts and behaviors. All will be required to conform to the dictates of "sacred technology."

Non-duality will be the new doctrine of the world religions. Religions will be one, gender becomes one, our thoughts and behaviors and responses to stimuli will become one. There will be blurred lines as to sexuality in greater degrees. Here are a few confusing titles: Transgender, bisexual, asexual, androgynous, gender binary, genderqueer, gender variant, and so forth. Individuality will be taboo and will not be allowed within the system. Individual thought or responses will be met with heavy disdain, penalty, or worse, punishment.

What sort of system would be so thorough and controlling, yet so enticing and rewarding to vast numbers of people in the world? What kind of system would be so appealing and acceptable to initiate demands of clamoring populations insisting on inclusion?

Let me tell you, who would demand involvement? A generation of computer and tech savvy populations who are comfortable with making technical tools and toys a literal extension of themselves. There is interest in the possibility of augmenting our brains; modulating our DNA; and using devices attached to our faces, heads, and bodies to increase our power by blending physically and mentally with our technology. We will become one with our machines.

We have an experienced generation of computer babies raised with tech toys, notepads, and cell phones. Whiz kids who are trained throughout childhood to become adept at computer use have now become adults who are connected to their technology 24-7. We cannot function without technology. It connects our families, homes, and communities.

As we move forward, ethical and moral decisions will be confronted as to how we manage AI (artificial intelligence) robots, avatars, and the huge data gathering process and associated technology industry being formulated at this moment.

Controversy will rage, but solutions will percolate. The truth is, you and I are "the product" in the new global technology paradigm, and our information will feed AI, "the data eating beast." Pandora's box is open. Science and technology are leapfrogging forward at an exponential pace. There is no mechanism to stop it...except God!

Putting on the full armor of God and reinforcing ourselves with a basic understanding of science and spiritual fact is necessary protection to carry us through the coming days of unbelievable technology.

> Finally, my brethren be strong in the Lord, and in the power of his might. Put on the whole armour of God, that ye may be able to stand against the wiles of the devil... Wherefore take unto you the whole armour of God, that ye may be able to withstand in the evil day, and having done all to stand" (Eph. 6:10–11, 13)

Chapter 3

We Wrestle Not against Flesh and Blood

As a grandmother, I flee from Satan and the occult world. But I am not so foolish as to deny or discount the powers and dark goals of the adversary. If we open ourselves to such things, there are demons and dark entities awaiting an invitation to enter our realm. Christ Himself interacted with and cast out demons. Demons recognized and feared His powers in resolving issues of demon possession.

> And straightway the father of the child cried out, and said with tears, Lord, I believe; help thou mine unbelief. when Jesus saw that the people came running together, he rebuked the foul spirit, saying unto him, Thou dumb and deaf spirit, I charge thee, come out of him, and enter no more into him. And the spirit cried, and rent him sore, and came out of him; and he (the child) was as one dead; but Jesus took him by the hand and lifted him up; and he arose. (Mark 9:25–27)

God has given clear powerful instruction in how to defend oneself from the powers of evil in all circumstances. He stated, "The glory of God, is intelligence, or, in other words, light and truth. Light and truth, forsake that evil one" (D&C 93:36–37). Our protection is found in accepting and becoming like Christ.

Satan has his counterfeit kingdoms. In the demonic realm, there are powers and status attributed to Santa's followers. Some have acquired greater importance and knowledge. There is a hierarchy of ruling classes among Satan's followers.

With the modern resurgence of evil and imbalance of right and wrong closing around us, we might need to reassess our adversary. Satan is organizing his plan for the coming millennial event. We need to wake up to this jarring possibility. My personal distaste of occult activity and its presence in the world does not change the fact that many from the time of Adam have recognized and practiced the dark arts. From the beginning, Satan was the opposer and enemy of God and man.

Satan's regime and a plethora of false gods have plagued all cultures. The great empire nations of Egypt, Assyria, Persia, and Babylon fell into the practice of worshipping kings and emperors laying upon them contrived godly powers. The Greeks and Romans assigned godhood and unwarranted honor to unnumbered human and animal forms.

Even today, secret societies and religious practitioners dedicate themselves to Satan and the occult. These malefactors are pushing forward their ancient plan. They are working for a return of past occult golden ages. The plan of Satan is to thwart and deter the final plan of the Father in establishing His Son to rule for a thousand years of peace.

Satan's minions also await the miraculous return of their honored kings and warriors. They await the return of power players and practitioners of the "craft." They await the release of the fallen angels, and devils held back by the restraining powers of God.

As bizarre as this sounds to rational people, the new technologies now available give these occult believers encouragement. Using the new quantum computers, scientists claim to have entered unknown dimensions and harvested resources. The claim is that certain frequencies resonate at particular levels, opening portals to angelic realms. The formula is, energy + wavelength = portal opening. The accurate wavelength, frequency, and power must be coalesced to allow quantum computers in sync with beam energies employed at the CERN Large Hadron Collider to open portals into other realms.

Science, in its attempt to open alternate portals, could present us with a tsunami of spirit entities flooding into our reality, perhaps the awaited return to our world of the "old ones." Those with forbidden knowledge as taught and believed by satanic secret societies throughout time. If technology is coming from the occult side and is the linchpin of the beast system, the system is demonic.

The ancient "science of the craft" is the dark arts from the days of Cain originating through Satan. Cain and his descendants manipulated stolen knowledge dispensed by rogue angels to enhance their dark goals. Magicians and sorcerers seeking power and hidden knowledge through divination claimed communication with fallen angels. This foundational knowledge may have slipped into modern-day science and technology through a small circle of believers practicing divination and modern-day necromancy.

Early scientist, H.P. Lovecraft, was a Satan worshipper and claimed to entertain fallen angels. He spoke to the great "Old Ones." In the sixteenth century, scientists John Dee and Edward Kelly claimed to be spirit mediums. They reported ancient math and language was revealed to them by spirits. The language was recorded in their personal journals. Dee's writings on the subject are extensive. When Carl Sagan wrote his novel, *Contact*, he acknowledged a higher intelligence communicated with humans through advanced mathematics. Scientist John Nash admitted communicating with alien assistance when coming up with his "Nash equilibrium theory" (Book *Revising Reality*, Anthony Patch and associates).

Hidden math and language in sync with occult rituals tapped into other realms by early scientists may be operating in our day. Sounds crazy, but for those who read the scriptures and believe them to be the Word of God through His prophets, connections and openings in space sound familiar. In the Holy Scriptures, God tells us of His stretched-out curtains and veils that separate earth from heaven.

Jacob, of the Bible, saw in a night vision angels moving up and down on a ladder of pure light. They descended and ascended through a portal or opening in the heavens above him.

We will shortly meet with Geordie Rose, CEO and founder of the new quantum computers originating out of British Columbia. He recently admitted an attempt to force energy properties into another dimension. He claims he succeeded in poking into a parallel dimension. When asked about the result, he stated there was a return of energy, Enochian math, and unknown properties. He sent through 100 percent energy and received back 110 percent, so unknown properties were returned into our dimension. When receiving unidentified resources from alternate dimensions, Anthony Patch calls the 10 percent mystery properties "quantum pollution" entering our reality. Could spiritual entities, DNA, or bacteria slip through such openings? We don't know. According to Anthony Patch, a macro sol portal could occur. In attempting to open God's space portals, D-Wave and CERN could open a permanent solar highway.

There was a twenty-year scientific exploration and data gathering probe of Saturn. The robotic spacecraft, Cassini, was launched October 15, 1997, and streamed data to scientists on earth. On September 13, 2019, the study was ended through a controlled death dive into the atmosphere of Saturn, disposing of the probe spacecraft. Huge amounts of data resulted from this endeavor. The Saturn Cassini probe measured magnetic fields and gravity of the planet and performed measuring and calibration. They examined the chemical composition of the atmosphere and sent back data and information concerning this ringed planet. Scientists have marked specific points on the poles of Saturn.

The north pole of Saturn is a naturally occurring hexagon shape and behaves as a synchrotron collider. Powerful winds cause curricular motion of high speed counter-circulating wind movement caused by intense Birkland currents at the north pole of Saturn. The south pole serves as a receiver.

The north and south poles of Saturn are connected through the core of the planet by a twisted spiral helix-shaped electrical energy known as the Birkeland currents. Birkeland currents appear naturally in the wide expanse of the cosmos. The question is, can a manufactured Birkeland current conduit originating from the LHC open and connect with the south pole of Saturn? Possibly. If so, the man-made establishment of a plasma conduit will be observed in the sky and be seen like the Norway spiral. It will show bright colors bolder than the aurora borealis affecting the entire magnetosphere. It will be northern lights on steroids. No one will miss it.

Birkeland currents will be energized by plasma excitation and become an ignited conduit through which strangelets will be propelled into the universe at designated targets.

The south pole of Saturn is a prime target. Some scientists and many Satan worshippers believe there is a "phantom zone" at the center of Saturn in which the fallen angels are imprisoned. Scientists at CERN have a quiet agenda to target this point and release the "fallen angels."

The dark purpose here is to reconstitute ancient DNA and summon the Antichrist spirit into our reality and then fashion him a hybrid human form. Ancient mummies and bodies preserved through involved preparation can possibly be restored. The DNA properties of human remains kept dry and protected can be viable for thousands of years. Total interaction and communication with ancient dead ones will require methods of bringing them from other dimensions into our reality, fashioning them host bodies, supported by specific digitized DNA. As you read on, you will be surprised as I am that these things are part of future technology.

Some scientists at CERN and dedicated Satanists are aware of this occult belief. God stated the fallen angels would be locked up until the time of end when they would no longer be restrained. So…

1. Will spirits of fallen angels be released through scientific ingenuity?
2. Will their DNA be sequenced and their spirit entities be teleported from unknown dimensions into our reality?
3. Will newly fashioned human biological bodies host these intruders?

4. Will CERN use the D-Wave encryption to unlock the abyss located beneath the CERN building?
5. Will locusts and scorpion-like demons rise out of the abyss?

There are many who believe interaction with spirit entities are possible. Some portions of the population could become possessed by spirits entering from distant realms entering through open portals. We are being conditioned right now through movies and children's cartoons filled with characters, good and bad, coming from other worlds through portals and conduits from space to earth.

Most are not aware these things are becoming possible now or in the very near future. The technology is being fastened in place. These bizarre sci-fi scenarios are really becoming possible.

Satan has his own plan running in tandem with God's final plan to reintroduce Christ at the Second Coming. In fact, the counterfeit plans of Satan may initiate and bring to pass the very fulfillment of many end-time prophecies and desolations proclaimed by true prophets. Satan may be allowed to harness science and technology for his ends.

Many today study, follow, and secretly practice Satan worship. Satan copies God's platform of true worship and realizes the powers incorporated into the plan of God to save man is effective. Satan and his followers are in position and using the distorted components of truth to run offense. His avid followers honor black Sabbaths and rituals. They promote sacrifice and conjure up demons, they practice casting of spells, and they study dark scripture and ancient logs. They practice oaths, speaking to the dead, and impose secret combinations to gain power and control through murder.

> For we wrestle not against flesh and blood, but against principalities, against powers, against the rulers of darkness of this world, against spiritual wickedness in high places. We need to be acquainted with the terms: principalities, powers, rulers of darkness and spiritual wickedness in high places. (Eph. 6:10–13)

Principalities

I encourage you to take a close look at the corruption and dark underbelly of big government bureaucrats in all nations. There are legions of secretive agencies both private and public. Many are anti-American and New World Order advocates. The Wall Street moneymen fund their hidden agenda through corrupt centralized governments. The globalist millionaires come from about sixteen family blood lines that have carried wealth and power forward for millennia. This cabal governs the governed. Heads of state look to them for direction. At board meetings and private gatherings, they discuss their agendas for world domination. The ends justify the means. They have ample holdings and money, but their real goal is for increased power and control of world resources and populations.

This behavior brings to mind the "secret combinations" taught to Cain by Satan himself. The ancient formula was the process of getting gain through secret oaths, lies, deception, and finally Cain turned to murder. I realize these comments smack of conspiracy, but there is a foundation of truth that becomes obvious in this instance.

Powers

Look at the worldwide contributors forking over millions of dollars to participate in a new world order of technology and control of world populations.

Nine billion dollars have been invested in CERN since 2012, and the US has provided 542 million of that figure, not including the constant influx of donations of generous world patrons from 2012 and forward. What is the draw of the unending support for this institution to exceed their goals? The fundraising machine at CERN seeks out technology industries, governments, and wealthy investors throughout the world.

DARPA (Defense Advanced Research Projects Agency) is deeply involved in the testing at CERN in combination with D-Wave computer company out of British Columbia. DARPA is at the heart of some of the most significant technological advances of our time.

The CIA and NSA have given grants for several million each. The Natural Science Foundation is funneling our tax dollars to venture capital investors, secular industry, and technology companies where 90 percent of all this funding goes for technology discovery.

The interlocking web of quietly involved governments, tech companies, universities, science institutions, and numerous peripheral millionaires is mind boggling. It is possible and very likely huge amounts of taxpayer monies are being diverted into the clandestine technology world with no accountability.

Military, industry, and technological science make a formidable trio. All of these entities are necessary, practical, and supportive of world societies. However, are they always benevolent? President Dwight D. Eisenhower left us a chilling message, "Beware the military industrial complex." One only has to follow the money to uncover the activity of the "military, industrial, technology complex" in the US and big governing players in the world at large. Follow the money, because a good deal of it is yours.

Rulers of Darkness

Be aware there are secret societies and foundations, deep states institutions, and improperly managed courts filled with corruption. These units can choose to rule over us in darkness and secrecy. Deep state structures can implement agendas and assume power in secret. Governing bodies can now implement precise surveillance using security systems for the purpose of population control. Modern technical mechanisms are in place to accomplish such an agenda.

When control, power, and tyranny are concerned, these could become malevolent masters. There is a great following and exceedingly wealthy groups that keep modern science and technology funded and moving forward. Contributions flow freely from the rich and famous also from national governments and world leaders intent on finding their place in a future world system.

Spiritual Wickedness in High Places

Social fiefdoms and the self-assigned elite circulate among the world societies, some under the protective mantle of religious-based authority. Great world churches ruled over by revered appointees who are given royal, holy status and allowed permission and control of vast adoring followers.

These chosen ones surround themselves with paid underling ministers who feed off the church contribution plates. This support cadre assists in the management of vast lay members—members that support the structure through financial offerings. Many of these powerful holy men rule countries, some rule the religious airways. All gain substantial wealth from these high positions. They practice priest craft, saving souls for money. Priest craft is religion for hire. Worshipping God is free.

Openly practicing satanic followers multiply among us. Masonry comes out of the ancient secret societies, including the alchemists, the Templars, the Cabbalists, Rosicrucian, the Knights of the Golden stone, the magicians and diviners, and, of course, the Luciferians, worshipping Satan.

Satan's rebellion was so intractable God had to cast him out of heaven; he and his followers were cast into the ambient regions of our earth. In this environment, he could embark on his quest to tempt men. He and his followers could carry out their plans to deceive those who were righteous and obedient to God. Some humans have chosen to be under the strong influence of those cast out along with Satan. Many mortals are unaware that they are being used. They are not necessarily possessed, as the Bible shows some are, but influenced by demons to act against our best interests.

A factor which God wants us to realize more completely and fully is that we are not alone in this ocean of air. Even as vicious sharks and barracuda prowl the water, their demonic counterparts, symbolized as fouls and unclean raptors and carrion eaters, inhabit the ocean of air right along with us. It is essential to our spiritual well-being to heed Paul's warning in the following scripture:

> Put on the whole *armour of God, that ye may be able to stand against the wiles of the devil. For we *wrestle not *against *flesh and blood, but against principalities, against powers, against the *rulers of the *darkness of this world, against spiritual *wickedness in high places. Wherefore take unto you the whole armour of God that ye may be able to withstand in the evil day, and having done all, to stand. (Eph. 6:11–13)

The demons hate us because we are followers of Christ. Satan knows this earth, our inheritance, will be given to the righteous sons of God. Satan is a master at the art of deception and uses these tools with great expertise. Most people in this world do not know they are deceived or how they became deceived. Satan and his minions have not sat us all down to tell us, "We are here to deceive you." Satan's time is short, and he is very aware of this fact. He will continue encouraging men to sin thereby forfeiting their redemption. However, through God-given agency, we can make choices. The battle is between good and evil, happiness and sorrow, darkness and light. Choose Christ. Those choosing Satan have traded agency for captivity.

We are not aware of Satan's unseen forces and equally unaware of guardian angels and deceased family members attempting to protect, comfort, and influence us for good. Be courageous and stand firm. Satan will continue to muddy the waters and trick humanity into committing sin and thereby forfeit their personal redemption.

What we must remember is that Elohim and His Son Jesus Christ are all powerful. We are holy creations with the ability to attune to the light of Christ. We are hardwired to God. He knows us and desires to lead us. It is up to each person to choose to seek the light and attune to the saving plan of the Savior. Satan's plan is one of coercion and death. Choose Christ and live.

God is not impotent or unaware of all players in the final game of chess. He holds all the pieces and runs the board. He is in control of all kings, queens, devils, and angels. The final game is His to win.

In this day, we have the insight and power of a true prophet leading us. The following is a prophetic promise from a modern-day prophet: "I bless you with the power to detect the adversary's deception, I bless you with greater capacity to receive revelation, and I bless you to be able to feel the infinite reach of God's perfect love for you" (Pres. Russel M. Nelson, 9/17/19, *BYU Devotional*).

Come Ye Out of Babylon

We live in the best of times and the worst of times. The ancients living in Babylon also lived in the best of times and the worst of times. Let's compare:

Babylon was a high-tech city of the time. The hanging gardens of Babylon were a marvel. The protective walls of Babylon were so thick and wide chariot races were held three or four abreast along the top of the wall. Theirs was a time of considerable technology. They excelled in shipping, trade, architectural abilities, merchandising, and tremendous wealth. The elite ruling classes had it all.

The term Babylon not only signifies a location, but it also signifies a state of being. In God's terms, Babylon incorporates all the corruption, evil, and affliction perpetrated upon man by the governing elite and overlords of huge cities. It denotes deep wickedness and perversion among unrepentant societies.

We in the United States could be living in America and also living in a Babylonian state of wickedness. Many are unaware. Could this revealing description of ancient Babylon, as pointed out by Dr. Hugh Nibley, awaken us to our dangerous dilemma?

The leaders had ample opportunity: Babylon offered it all for a price. She had cargos of gold, silver, precious stones, and pearls; clothiers who produced fine linen, purple, silk, and scarlet cloth; furniture makers had home decorators who fashioned citron wood and made articles of ivory, bronze, iron, and marble. The list goes on. She was the great supermarket carrying cinnamon and spices, incense, myrrh, frankincense, wine, oil, fine flour and wheat, cattle and sheep; her transportation department included horses and carriages.

Finally, she offered as slaves the very souls of men. Babylon seeks to reduce people to flesh that can be bought and sold for profit. In the conquest, men are dehumanized by the consorts of Babylon. This idea is brought out by the last phrase "souls of men." This is an old Hebrew phrase depicting men as "little more than human livestock." This last commodity shows the spiritual depth of Babylon's wickedness. She sold human beings, old and young, male and female. Their lives were to be drained away to provide more for those whose fortunes were already so vast that not even the most lavish expenditures could deplete them. "Humans became a commodity."

These are soul-jarring truths and certainly apply to the modern practices of abortion and the selling of baby body parts, and what of the forced sex trade trafficking that is rampant throughout America today? I am struck by our evil mirroring of the sins of Babylon. Welcome to Babylon.

John the Revelator explains that Babylon's seductive power tempts almost everyone. In the face of this reality, the angel gives a command and warning: "Come out of her, my people that ye receive not of her plagues" (Rev. 18:4).

The saints in the latter days have received the same warning. The voice of the Lord is unto you: "Go ye out of Babylon; gather ye out from among the nations, from the four winds, from one end of heaven to the other" (D&C 133:7). And more explicitly, "Go ye out from among the nations, even from Babylon from the midst of wickedness which is spiritual Babylon" (D&C 133:14).

The Lord means for His followers to take him seriously; he warns, "After today cometh the burning—this is speaking after the manner of the Lord—for verily I say, tomorrow all the proud and they that do wickedly shall be as stubble; and I burn them up, for I am the Lord of Hosts, and I will not spare any that remain in Babylon" (D&C 64:24).

Chapter 4

God's Truth Overrides Deception

There are many who deceive and the spectrum of deception is broad. (Lawrence E. Corbridge, *BYU Magazine*, Summer 2019)

For in those days (our day) there shall also arise false Christs and false prophets, and shall show great signs and wonders, insomuch, that, if possible, they shall deceive the very elect, who are the elect according to the covenant. (Matt. 24:24)

Men are not hungry for knowledge. They are hungry for truth. The questionable truth of our day is a barrage of nonstop sound bites, intrusive ads, and technology-based distractions offering knowledge on every possible topic.

Before we drown in information, we must realize that not all knowledge is the same. There is a hierarchy among the things you and I must learn. Not all information and knowledge is of equal value. Perhaps we could augment scientific learning through spiritual revelation.

There are four different methods of learning—namely, the scientific, analytical, academic, and divine methods. The divine method of learning incorporates elements of the other three but ultimately trumps everything else by tapping into the powers of heaven.

Ultimately, the things of God are made known by the Spirit of God, which is usually a still, small voice. The Lord said, "God shall give unto you knowledge by his Holy Spirit, yea, by the unspeakable gift of the Holy Ghost" (D&C 121:26). "All four methods are necessary to know the truth. They all begin the same way; with a question. Questions are worth pursuing" (Lawrence E. Corbridge, *BYU Magazine*, Summer 2019).

Questions addressed to God in our sincere prayers are answered in every righteous area of endeavor.

> We learn that over the sweep of centuries, God has released a divine dispensing of restorative doctrines and scripture as circumstances and faith have allowed. Truths are pouring out of the heavens, apocryphal writings and ancient records are pushing up out of the earth. Modern day scriptures have come forth and the world is awash with evidence of God. God is giving away the spiritual secrets of the universe…but are we listening? (Neal Maxwell)

We live in a Golden Age of learning. We have a lot to learn in a short time. God has given us a very fertile field in which to cultivate our knowledge and support great outcomes. It seems to me a priority would be to seek knowledge about the true God. That critical knowledge and information is available and accessible to those who desire to know. Men's study of quantum science requires a rudimentary understanding of the workings of the True God of the Universe.

The Godhead

The most valuable truth ever sought or found in this wide universe is a basic understanding of the Godhead.

> And this is life eternal that they might know thee, the only true God and Jesus Christ whom thou hast sent. (John 17:3)

The trinity consists of separate beings but of one mind and one purpose with one result, "To bring to pass the immortality and eternal life of man."

The Father and the Son are resurrected, glorified beings with bodies of flesh and bone filled with infinite measures of truth, light, intelligence, and power. The Holy Ghost is a personage of spirit without a body. The core make up of all three members of the Godhead is inherent light, truth, and intelligence. These three elements are foundational in "spirit matter," and all three members of the trinity can draw out of that great reservoir of spiritual matter, also called the Light of Christ to create, to enlighten our minds, and to reveal truth to us.

The Holy Ghost can be called the Holy Spirit as a title, but do not confuse him with the noun Holy Spirit when referring to the great spiritual matter component that is used by the Godhead individually and as a whole in the process of creation.

Awareness of God's truth and the truths found in science necessarily dovetail. This combined knowledge is not only informative but also transformative.

With so much peripheral junk data, we can become unfocused, confused, and weary. Many people in the world are laboring under this overwhelming construct. Timothy addresses this in the following scripture: "Men are ever learning, and never able to come to the knowledge of the truth" (2 Tim. 3:7).

Our modern scientists are tripping into God's domain. I am asking you to read and consider the rich unappreciated theory that I call God Science. I am asking you to open your heart and mind to the actual God particle and its cosmic functionality and basis for all existence.

Some regard scripture and prophecy as mythical fantasies, and some regard the scriptures as fact. I regard the God of the universe as a glorified, resurrected being, and His words are indeed fact.

The creative prowess, spiritual and scientific expertise of an all-powerful God, places Him in the center of creation. He is the master of all physical laws, intelligence, control of universal creation and cosmic governance.

The greatest scoffers and deniers are found among the science and technology scholars.

God's divinely created architecture connecting man, earth, solar system, galaxy, and universe is so precise we must "cease and desist" in disturbing this critical balance. The true God holds everything in perfect balance, from the wide macro universe down to the nuclear subatomic level. He has established a plan that will support human life on infinite earths throughout His dominions. God will protect and support His architecture, but there is a growing threat that could initiate a destructive imbalance on this earth. This threat is birthed through misapplied science and technology.

> By the word of the Lord were the heavens made; and all the host of them by the breath of his mouth. He gathereth the waters of the sea together as an heap: he layeth up the depth in storehouses. Let all the earth fear the Lord: let all the inhabitants of the world stand in awe of him. For he spake, and it was done; he commanded, and it stood fast. (Ps. 33:6–9)

A recent scientific discovery the breaking news of the God particle rocked the scientific world. I will thoroughly discuss this astounding scientific breakthrough, but I want to present you with a relatively unrecognized eternal paradigm shift concerning elemental matter. What we learn about matter really matters!

The technological future is unsettling, but truth brings rationality and calm. Some additional truths found in scripture overrides modern science and provides missing puzzle pieces that bring needed strength and knowledge fitting us for the times we live in.

A combination of new knowledge and increased spiritual understanding will bring greater consciousness. Humans are the one creation who can be endowed with greater intelligence. We can expand our spiritual and mental context as we escape the mental confinements of earthly language and thinking.

You and I accept all kinds of scientific theory, until a theory is proven misguided or patently wrong. In the following paragraphs, I am asking you to consider a remarkable all-encompassing theory. It will not only meet the strong testing of skeptics and believers over time but also support and enhance the new science and technology advances of our day.

As you move forward, I will do my best to explain the basics of this rich theory and how it relates to the science and technology of our time. I present God's implementation and use of the true God Particle to be a solid foundational theory embedded in what I reverently call God Science.

The "God Science" theory may prove shocking to some who have never heard of or been taught of this wonderful, self-explaining, mind-expanding truth. Many in the field of science and even some involved in religion are adamantly opposed to even the mention of these two studies (science and religion) intermingling.

As we move forward together in this study, you may feel overwhelmed and at times find this journey is brain stretching. Let's stretch! Now we will begin a God Science introduction that is a beautiful blending with the worthy discovery and expertise of our modern scientists. They have made remarkable findings in the area of science, modern technology, and particle physics. The noteworthy discovery of the Higgs Boson deserves the accolades and the world recognition it received.

Atoms Emit Light

All things are made up of atoms. Atoms have two parts. A heavy matter part called a fermion and a mirror image invisible part called a boson. The boson always appears to emit light so it has the qualities of a photon.

In study of the duality of the atom, the fermion building material is as diverse as countless variations of heavy matter throughout space. The antimatter twin image is what God calls intelligence or spiritual matter. This spirit matter is rich in properties of love, light, and intelligence, and also extends throughout space. When these forms of matter come together, the binding material is always a photon, which is light. This binding property is called a boson.

We cannot find an atom, subatomic particle or functioning system throughout universal space, but that light has something to do with it. Perhaps the photon or light is likely the only part of spiritual matter we can see, and even then our eyes see only a tiny sliver of the extensive light scale. (See image of the light scale diagram.)

THE LIGHT OF CHRIST

Sunlight	Instinct	Human Reason	Light of the Gospel	Light of the Celestial Kingdom
-Quickens life in the plant kingdom	-Quickens life among birds, animals, fish, insects	-Quickens man -Analysis -Reason -Judgment	Regenerating -Power given to faithful -Power of Holy Ghost and Priesthood	-All knowledge -All understanding -All use of law, love, power, glory, Dominion, Eternal increase, power to become Gods -Creators

The Light of Christ

The light of Christ is a divine energy, power or influence that proceeds from God through Jesus Christ and gives light and life to all things. It is the law by which all things are governed in heaven and earth. It also helps us understand gospel truths and places us on the road to exaltation.

The light which is in all things, which giveth
life to all things, which is the law by which all things
are governed, even the power of God who sitteth

upon his throne, who is in the bosom of eternity, who is in the midst of all things. (D&C 88:13)

This light (photon) is part of the powerful intelligence and energy that is inherent in God Himself and is also in everything He creates. He has revealed this superpower from the beginning of time. The true God Particle is intelligence! What is intelligence?

Intelligence is the main component in spiritual matter, a companion attached to heavy, temporal matter. Together they form everything that is created by God. This rich spirit matter formula is placed in every creation, especially in man. Many call it the Light of Christ or the Spark. "That he (Christ) was the true light, which lighteth every man that cometh into the world. 10) He was in the world and the world was made by Him, and the world knew Him not..." (John 1:9–10).

Two Forms of Matter

The prophet Joseph Smith explained this principal in DC 131:7–8: "There is no such thing as immaterial matter, all spirit is matter, but it is more pure and can only be discerned by purer eyes we cannot see it; but when our bodies are purified, we shall see that it is all matter."

The *Book of Mormon* gives us a beautiful, clear description of the two forms of matter.

> And now, my sons, I speak unto you these things for your profit and learning; for there is a God, and he hath created all things, both the heavens and the earth, and all things that in them are, both things to act and things to be acted upon. (2 Nephi 2:14)

Now we see there are things to act and things to be acted upon called eternal elements. It is all matter. Joseph Smith said that matter existed in two forms (duality). The very refined element is called Spirit, and the coarse element is called temporal matter. So it is that all matter exists in different states. It is like ice and water. They are really the same thing, but they are in different forms. Now everything is made up of a combination of these two forms of matter. These are the building blocks of the universe. (See Abraham 4:10, 12, 18 in the *Pearl of Great Price* scripture; also see *Book of Mormon*, Helaman 12:8–9.)

The universe is dual. These two realms are closely interwoven and perhaps come from the same ultimate source, yet they are distinct in their nature. These building blocks are coeternal and coexistent with God and have always been in place and will always be available.

Remember, there are things to act and things to be acted upon. This is a critical creation process used by the gods.

Building Blocks in Space

The unorganized universe is a repository of primal building blocks. There is an unlimited number of unorganized elements—heavy temporal matter and invisible spirit matter.

God did not create out of nothing (ex-nihilo). All things are formed from preexisting materials, which are the two universal building blocks, intelligent spirit matter and temporal matter. These were things to act and things to be acted upon. The intelligent matter has the capacity to act upon temporal matter.

These two forms of matter exist in unimaginable abundance. These are God's basic building materials. God has mastery over them and over His holy construction. His relationship to His organized, completed creations merge in an enduring, eternal connection. He is ever vigilant and mindful of his handiwork.

The normal state of matter is chaos. The normal state of God is organization and perfect order through law. These unorganized building blocks exist in a natural crude state, waiting for God's power to sweep them up and organize them. God can requisition these building blocks and create worlds, solar systems, galaxies, and universes, then populate them with His greatest creation—human life. God spoke, "For by the power of my Spirit created I them; yea, all things both spiritual and temporal" (D&C 29:31).

Temporal and Spiritual Matter

The things we can see are forms of temporal matter, but the parts we know are there but we cannot see are "spiritual matter."

Spirit matter is the purest, most refined and subtle of all substances, and the one least understood or even recognized by the less informed among mankind. It is the spiritual power essence managed and applied in differing degrees by each member of the Godhead. This powerful component is available to the Trinity.

Let's describe spirit matter because it has the ability to act upon elemental matter, which is inert.

Intelligence is a key component of "spirit matter," and this spirit matter formula is inseparably associated with every particle of elemental matter. So these particles are diffused throughout the system in which they dwell. Each is separate and apart from each other having levels of intelligence, and "collectively" even greater levels of intelligence. Each must be able to acknowledge and obey the required laws in its sphere. There are gradations of intelligence among the collective mass.

Spirit matter is the active agency by which God rules His massive dominions. Spirit matter is the great controlling matter of all other elements. Subordinate elements submit to this superior property. God's universe is a great repository of these two great primary forms of matter. It is abundant and ever present. This spiritual formula is invisible to our mortal organs, but its operations deeply affect our being.

God speaks to this sea of intelligent particles and instructs portions to take up residence in particles of temporal matter. The finely prepared temporal matter with the prescribed levels of intelligent matter can then perform assigned functions. Without this combination of elements, the universe and all that is in it would be without form and void.

God pairs together particles containing intelligence with portions of temporal elements. They are paired in complex but orderly ways; they are assigned functions, roles, and must abide by the physical and spiritual laws of God's universe. Some intelligence is paired with plant life, some with animal life, and superior levels of intelligence is paired with the human element, our temporal bodies. Other intelligences are paired with nonorganic elements.

These intelligences are independent and act voluntarily. They are not compelled, and the heavens wait on them until they obey. They don't do anything until they are ready, just like we. And our Heavenly Father built the whole universe with this agency of action. This energy factor in the universe is intelligence, and it only operates as fast and in a direction it is willing to follow. See D&C 93:30.

Now these intelligences are graded from the lowest to the highest, and the highest of all is God's intelligence Himself, and we are in between. Some intelligent matter was assigned to plant life, and some was assigned to animals. Those that were His very special, superior, and superdeluxe intelligences were given bodies in His image, and you are one of them. You are very special people. (See Abraham 3:19.)

If you were a scientist, this will be exciting information because our most advanced research scientists have just proven this is true. Matter does not function mechanically. It has an element of finite intelligence, they say. That's what Bergson, the French philosopher, called it. It can distinguish. It can choose. It doesn't always do what the rules say. Some of those little elements are just as ornery as you and I. They go wandering around, and it is the aggregate that upholds the law of chemistry. In the aggregate, yes, but you look at them individually, and they are fooling around. As a matter of fact, Robert Millikan said, "If all the elements were obeying all the rules of chemistry you would never die. There is rebellion in the flesh and it is called Seeds of Death."

> Again, verily I say unto you, he hath given a law unto all things, by which they move in their times and their seasons. (D&C 88:42)

> All kingdoms have a law given. And there are many kingdoms; for there is no space in which there is no kingdom; and there is no kingdom in which there is no space, either a greater or a lesser kingdom. And unto every kingdom is given a law; and unto every law there are certain bounds also and conditions. All creation adheres to God's law. (D&C 88:36–38)

The scriptures tell us God combines primary spirit matter with secondary temporal matter. Without this added-upon God formulae, the universe and all that is in it would be "without form and void."

At God's command, temporal elements that have received intelligence attached to them will obey. You want a mountain to move, talk to it. God commands it, or His Priesthood does it by His authority. When God commands, the dual combination of elements obey. (See Jacob 4:6 and 1 Nephi 20:23.)

Let's talk about the visible world. We see stars, trees, grass, animals, birds, clouds, children, people, and all tangible creation. That is temporal matter. However, to exist in a God-created form, this heavy temporal matter requires an infused counterpart of intelligent matter to take on the form, shape, and life God desires.

Listen to Brigham Young discussing this principle:

> There is light or intelligence in all matter throughout the vast extent of all the eternities. It is in the rock. It is in the sand, in water and air. It is in the gases and, in short, in every description or organization of matter, whether it be solid,

liquid, or gas. We begin to catch the vision of this miracle of God's creation. He goes into outer darkness of unorganized intelligences and unorganized bits of temporal matter and combines them together so that a little tiny bit of temporal matter has an "intelligence" attached to it, and now He can command it. The Lord has said, I have given all of them a pattern which becomes the law by which they operate.

Plants need to respond to the laws of photosynthesis to grow, animals must respond to instinct to reproduce, planets, stars, and space creations must adhere to the constructs of rotation and orbiting law.

Intelligence is the key component of spirit matter, and this spirit matter formula is inseparably associated with every particle of temporal matter. These particles are diffused throughout the system in which they dwell. Each is separate and apart from each other having different levels of intelligence, and "collectively" even greater levels of intelligence. Each must be able to acknowledge and obey the required laws in its sphere. There are gradations of intelligence among the collective mass.

It pervades all things. It is in and through all things in universal space. It is intimately associated with light, intelligence, and truth. It also incorporates the primal life force, priesthood law, and all godly attributes are found therein. It is responsive to the direction, command, and power of God's voice, thereby obeying His commands.

It is what Tesla called the pervasive electric plasma. It is also the Higgs Field and dark matter, improperly named by science today.

Earth Creation

"And were it possible that man could number the particles of the earth, yea, millions of earths like this, it would not be a beginning to the number of thy creations; and thy curtains are stretched out still; and yet thou art there, and thy bosom is there; and also thou are just, and merciful and kind forever" (Moses 7:30). See *Pearl of Great Price* scripture.

We actually live in the midst of two universes. The unorganized portion, like time, is without beginning or end. It continues outward in every direction. It extends beyond the reach of our most powerful telescopes. Our Latter-day Saint prophet, Joseph Smith, stated early on that we live in an expanding universe. Science validates that theory.

As soon as God enters the explosive, chaotic environs of the unorganized universe, He carves out and establishes an organized space of order and embarks on creating. Those who hold the power and omnipotence of God can requisition mold and handle temporal matter and the highly refined spiritual matter as easily as we can mold and shape clay.

God speaks to this sea of intelligent particles and instructs portions to take up residence in particles of temporal matter. The finely prepared combination has the precise levels of intelligence to then perform assigned functions and adhere to prescribed law.

> Again, verily I say unto you, he hath given a law unto all things, by which they move in their times and their seasons; And their courses are fixed, even the courses of the heavens and the earth, which comprehend the earth and all the planets, and they give light to each other in their times and in their seasons, in their minutes, in their hours in their days in their weeks, in their months, in their years. (D&C 88:42–44)

Even God Himself must adhere to the structured laws of the universe. The Father explains He walks the razor's edge of celestial law continually in order to maintain the confidence and honor of all those who trust Him. Honor is the source of His power. If He were ever to be capricious, unjust, arbitrary or false in any sense, the plan would fail. He works within very strict rules and laws. He functions so that He never could violate any confidence or destroy the trust of all who depend on Him. The honor extended to Him by every creation in His dominions is His power. (See full document, the Cleon Skousen paper, "The Meaning of the Atonement.")

The key to modern physics and astronomy were taught from the beginning to Adam and many of God's prophets down through time. Writing the *Book of Abraham* made Joseph Smith a scientist far ahead of his time. Many new breakthroughs in modern science can be found in the writings of Abraham, Job, and Joseph Smith.

The prophet, Joseph Smith, was taught an important scientific principle. He stated, "This earth is organized or formed out of the remains of other planets that were broken up and recast into this earth on which we live. When elements in an organized form do not fill the measure of their creation they are thrown back to be made over again. The cosmic abundance of temporal elements can be used over and over again."

> Gods are continually recycling stellar elements of the universe. They are decontaminated, refurbished, and reused. They are used until these elements meet their potential and are permanently associated with eternal cosmic organizations. Some planets have gone on to perfection and other planets have gone out of existence through self-destruction." (President Spencer Kimball)

> The earth rolls upon her wings, and the sun giveth his light by day, and the moon giveth her light by night, and the stars also give their light, as they roll upon their wings in their glory, in the midst of the power of God. Unto what shall I liken these kingdoms, that ye may understand? Behold, all these are kingdoms, and any man who hath seen any or the least of these hath seen

God moving in his majesty and power. (D&C 88:45–47)

Example: In the small kingdom of atoms, there is a nucleus with protons and electrons orbiting around this active controlling center. This construct is the same moving into larger kingdoms such as rotating earths, solar systems, and galaxies.

A Star Is Born

And God said, "Let there be light: and there was light." (Gen. 1:3)

Scientists call light imponderable matter, because after pondering it, they have no answer for its pervasive presence. Light includes the visible light we see with our eyes, as well as the infinite electromagnetic spectrum and the higher level spiritual reaches of holy revelatory super energy light that surrounds deity.

However, spiritual matter is endowed with the primal life force, intelligence, and light. Light is the photon and is electromagnetic in nature. It is very possible light is the unifying medium for all known physical and quantum forces. The Scriptures teach often about the supernal Light associated with God the Father and His Son Jesus Christ, the Light of Christ. These light powers are in reference to the pure, invisible, and all-permeating spirit matter that fills the universe.

The light we can see and feel is the heated light radiating from our sun. It is the conduit providing nourishment and warmth for plant life, animal life, and survival of the human race. There are two basic theories as to the source of the heat and light supporting our sun.

Science fact: The Bethe-Gamow theory states the sun is suffering a heat death from inside. When the burning fuels of hydrogen properties are gone, the sun will die out like a used candle. In this state, temperatures should be greater at the center of the sun, but this is not the case. There are far greater temperatures at the outer edge of the sun in the halo or corona surrounding it.

Science fact: The scientist Fred Hoyle offers us the Hoyle theory of accretion. He postulates our sun is drawing light, heat, and energy from outside itself, perhaps a source even outside our galaxy. From modern scripture in the *Pearl of Great Price*, we learn from ancient writings of Abraham that the Hoyle theory is correct. This record speaks of a cosmic unending supply of solar energy that originates from the governing stars at the center of God's dominion. From this same God-centered system, there seems to be an authoritative chain of light and energy that is judiciously released so as not to burn up or freeze our sun. Energy and matter are directed toward our sun, which is absorbed through the process of accretion.

> And the light which shineth, which giveth you light, is through him who enlighteneth your eyes, which is the same light that quickeneth your understandings; Which light proceedeth forth from the presence of God to fill the immensity of space. The light which is in all things, which giveth life to all things, which is the law by which all things are governed, even the power of God who sitteth upon his throne, who is in the bosom of eternity, who is in the midst of all things. (D&C 88:11–13)

Stars and earths are actually born! They have planetary ancestry back to the great governing stars like the star, Kolob. Our earth belongs to a grouping attached to a cosmic hierarchy. "Kolob is the great star that governs all the earths belonging to the order in which our earth dwells" (*Pearl of Great Price*, chapter 3).

> And I, Abraham, had the urim and thummim, which the Lord my God had given unto me, in Ur of the Chaldees; And I saw the stars, that they were very great, and that one of them

was nearest unto the throne of God; and there were many great ones which were near unto it; And the Lord said unto me: These are the governing ones; and the name of the great one is Kolob, because it is near unto me, for I am the Lord thy God: I have set this one to govern all those which belong to the same order as that upon which thou standest. (Abraham 3:1–3)

Thus I, Abraham, talked with the Lord, face to face, as one man talketh with another; and he told me of the works which his hands had made; And he said unto me: My son, my son (and his hand was stretched out), behold I will show you all these. And he put his hand upon mine eyes, and I saw those things which his hands had made, which were many; and they multiplied before mine eyes, and I could not see the end thereof. (Abraham 3:11–12)

If two things exist, and there be one above the other, there shall be greater things above them; therefore Kolob is the greatest of all the Kokaubeam (stars) that thou hast seen, because it is nearest unto me. (Abraham 3:16)

Astronomers confirm our earth consists of the same variety of elements that are known to appear elsewhere in the observable universe. Every type of luminous matter emits a unique energy spectrum. (See stellar spectrum or interstellar matter.)

Human Creation

"And there stood one among them that was like unto God, and he said unto those who were with him: we will go down for there is space there, and we will take of these materials, (element and intelligence) we will make an earth whereon these (God's spirit children) may dwell" (Abraham 3:24). (See *Pearl of Great Price* scripture.)

God has created worlds without number for the purpose of placing His spirit children into mortality where they learn to manage the lower elements. Because of our combined elemental and spiritual bodies and our mortal experiences, we can practice fully the law of duality. With this duality, we obtain important choices. We choose right or wrong, light or dark, goodness or evil, hope or despair, and life or death. With duality comes infinite agency and choice. Bringing laws of duality and agency into sync, we can reach our individual potential to become like our Father, the awesome God, who created us.

God's great intelligence allows His personal mastering of this energetic field of spiritual and temporal matter. His powers keep His work secure and enduring. All lower and higher levels of creation respond to the voice frequency and innate powers of God. His relationship to His creations is fixed. It is as though we and all creations are "hardwired" to Him.

Humans are first and foremost spiritual entities, actually spirit sons and daughters of God. Our ultimate goal is to receive a mortal elemental body at birth. Our spirit is the template for our physical appearance. Mortal matter and spirit matter combine to make up the soul of man. We are not allowed to see our spiritual bodies at this time. Spirit matter can only be discerned by purer eyes.

Of course, man is the prime and single creation who has agency to choose, to reason, to assess situations, and to adjust to circumstances. Man is embedded with a superior gradation of spiritual matter. Man can respond to his native intelligence or seek after greater light and understanding. He is the one creation conditioned for increased enlightenment and endowments of greater knowledge. Man and all creation have the opportunity to progress in their sphere and "fill the measure of their creation."

We are His prized creation, and all other constructs were fashioned to bring us, His offspring, eventually home to Him. We are spiritually connected to our God and quantum entangled with Him.

God is very clear and direct that humans, like all creations, have His spirit in them. We carry God particles within us. We all receive the light of Christ as an inherent component of our human makeup. We are filled with intelligent spirit matter.

Intelligent spirit matter contains the primal life force. It cannot be destroyed or created. It is eternal! It provides the id of identity and the core personality. The self-existent ego under God's organizational powers can become embodied. This spiritual intelligent matter has many gradations and is of superior first order material. This order of matter has choice and freedom in its own sphere.

The first order is: organized intelligence and light, which forms spirit bodies.

The second order is: Spirit bodies combined with temporal element forms physical bodies.

Both of these bodies come through a process of birth. We are the literal spiritual children of God.

As with temporal matter, spirit matter cannot be created or destroyed. It is subject to organization and disorganization. Example: you can burn a piece of wood. Is the wood gone and destroyed? No. The wood has changed form. It is now ashes and gases. If we freeze water, the water is still there in a different form, namely ice.

If a person dies, is he destroyed forever? No. His form is changed at death. He lays down his heavy temporal matter body and retains his spirit matter body to resume existence as a spirit personage in another assigned dimension temporarily. All spirits good and evil return to prepared areas after death to await a restoration. Remember, these dual building blocks are indestructible.

Man has a dual, two-part nature. He straddles the spiritual and physical worlds. He has senses that operate in both spheres. As mortals, "We are not human beings having a spiritual experience; we are spiritual beings having a human experience."

The Second Law of Thermodynamics

This dual nature of all matter assures that our human bodies will be subject to the second law of thermodynamics (entropy) and will succumb to decomposition and decay when we experience death. We lay our bodies into the earth for a time. Our spirit body crosses over to another dimension. Our spirit body retains all our conscious thoughts, memories, personality, and intelligence. We cross from death to an afterlife for a temporary period.

We remain in this state until a point when God calls forth the very temporal matter that was ours in mortality. This element will be called forth—to be purified, sanctified, and glorified—by our creator and returned to us. This restoration of body and spirit results in beautiful, eternal resurrected bodies never to be separated again.

> Man was also in the beginning with God. Intelligence, or the light of truth, was not created or made, neither indeed can be… For man is spirit. The elements are eternal, and spirit and temporal element, inseparably connected, receive a fullness of joy; and when separated, man cannot receive a fullness of joy. (D&C 93:29, 33–34)

God practices a miraculous specificity for His children. Our gifts, talents, knowledge, life histories, and mortal experiences are recorded in our very cells. For this reason, we want our specified individual matter allotted to us at birth, bestowed back upon us as resurrected beings. Your history is precious and designated to you as my personal history is designated to me. It will be mine also, forever. Our very cells are encoded with our history.

Scientists and scholars access great reservoirs of knowledge. Often, they speak from a platform of knowing everything. However, when they speak of everything, they must consider first what things they are aware of, as well as those things of which they could be unaware. So scientists and students can only speak of the things they happen to know.

Possibly, the peculiarities pertaining to life and the particulars associated with deep thought lies outside the scope of basic science. We may need to seek for things provided in a spiritual context.

Two areas of discovery are critical and becoming more widely discussed. First, there is an organizing, ordering force in the universe that is active and runs counter to many established laws of science. Second, we have an awareness of "great gaps" in our knowledge that may account for our failure in science to discover the source of the force.

What is this strange force? Scientists don't know, but they see it working. Could it be the true God Particle intelligence?

Let's discuss the second law of thermodynamics. It states that everything in our universe eventually runs down. Left to itself, everything becomes more and more disorderly, until the final and natural state of things is a completely random distribution of matter. We accept this second law. In the course of nature, all matter takes a relentless journey of decomposition.

Book of Mormon scripture (2 Nephi 9:7 and Mosiah 16:10) tells us, "This corruption (could not) put on incorruption." Corruption of our physical bodies at death is a one-way process and seems irreversible. "Wherefore the first judgement, physical death came upon man and must needs have remained to an endless duration." Decay is always from heavier to lighter particles. So things decay and break down to smaller crumbling, rotting remains.

Any kind of order is unnatural and happens only by chance encounters. Highly organized events are statistically impossible. Humans have no business being here. We are not the natural order of things. Human life created out of a chaotic universe is against the natural flow of physical events. Scientists and naturalists agree that if nature has anything to say about it, we shouldn't be here. Life is a rare and unreasonable thing, the probability of it occurring and continuing is infinitesimal.

When I walk into a room that is in disarray and chaotic, and return later and find it in good order, I don't think time has backed up. I think some helpful intelligent person has tidied up that room.

When we observe dissolution and disorder of matter at various levels, we are observing the state of entropy. Tidy states of matter are far less common than untidy states of matter usually found in disarray.

There is a troubling dichotomy, if the relentless operation of the second law of thermodynamics breaks down all matter, then all things at the atomic level would now have decayed into lighter particles. But that clearly hasn't happened.

The Kemmerer theory states there is another force that tends toward symmetry and coherence. There seems to be a very exact law, which is preventing this total entropy or destruction. The renowned scientist, Buckminster Fuller, calls it syntropy.

All faithful seekers and interested Christians have access to personal revelation, which can augment scientific laws in ways that modern scientists reject and ridicule.

There is an exact law that overrides the law of harsh entropy. God promises an effective principal of unlimited application. An infinite principle is at work here. This dynamic law that overrides entropy is the process of resurrection through that precious act of the atonement. Atonement is the reversal of the degradative process, a returning of all humans and all creation to their former state, being integrated and reunited again…at one.

> Christ's ultimate gift is a retroactive and future promise of a restored resurrection of all creation and promised endowments of salvation placed upon the obedient. The magic force that saves us from entropy is Christ and the Father, both of whom are filled with maximum levels of intelligence, light, and truth. Theirs is a fullness of the rich spiritual formulae embedded in each of their creations. Embedded in each of us! If we accept the sacrifice made for all creation, we can become restored beings filled with the Light of Christ. (Paraphrased second law of thermodynamics by Parley P. Pratt, *Key to Theology*)

The First Law of Thermodynamics

The first law of thermodynamics is equally important. Nothing is lost, totally destroyed, or wasted. We and all of God's creations are indestructible and are made to last for eternities. This is the law of conservation of energy and matter. The world was organized out of the abundance of matter that fills the universe. It cannot be destroyed but can be acted upon and changed. There is an eternity of matter. Astronomers estimate there is between us and the nearest fixed stars, matter enough from which to organize millions of earths like this.

We are God's prized creation, and all other constructs were fashioned to bring us, His offspring, back into His presence. We are all children of God the Father. We lived with Him in a pre-earth life. We are all brothers and sisters and existed as spirit beings for possibly eons, as we were tutored and prepared for a time we would take on mortal bodies to enter our second estate. Now, as humans, we are in our second estate living on a temporal earth created for us by our elder brother, Jesus Christ. Christ was the agent, who, under the authority of the Father, was assigned to carry out the creation of this earth on which we dwell.

This creative operation was not new to God nor was the overall plan of salvation new. God the Father has many earths, and His saving plan is an eternal fully tested construct that produces the safest chance for redeeming his children. It is the eternal plan that has been and will be in place throughout the eternities.

> The Light of Christ is a divine energy, power of influence that proceeds from God through Jesus Christ and gives life and light to all things, It is the law by which all things are governed in heaven and earth. It also helps us understand gospel truths and places us on the road to exaltation. It also provides the primal life force. (Bruce R. McConkie, *Mormon Doctrine: Spirit of the Lord*, pp. 752)

PART 2

Titans of Technology

Chapter 5

Meet the D-Wave Team

D-Wave Company was founded in 1999. The founders are Geordie Rose and Haig Farris. It is a privately held company located in Burnaby, British Columbia.

The Money Pours In

D-Wave Company originated with a huge loan from DARPA (Defense Advanced Research Projects Agency). This is a US Department of Defense agency responsible for the development of emerging technologies for use by the military dollars. A Canadian public fund invested $30 million in 2017 and chooses to continue future investing. In the year of 2018, venture capital came pouring into D-Wave. In-Q-Tel donated seed capital. They were joined by NSA, University of California, Virginia Tech, Lockheed, Google, Amazon, Volkswagen, and Clarion Independence. They all work together in Silicon Valley, California. Of course, CERN is a critical supporter and partner with D-Wave Company. Work goes on at the Quantum Computer Artificial Intelligence Lab located at the CERN facility. This lab is an extension of National Aeronautics and Space Administration. Government, scientists, technology experts, and universities have an incestuous relationship involving technology.

Some of the buyers and owners of the D-Wave quantum computers are Google, NASA (National Aeronautics and Space Administration), USRA (University Space Research Association),

Lockheed Martin, Temporal Defense System, Virginia Tech, and many other universities. They can access D-Wave through remote locations. Jeff Bezos of Amazon; Elon Musk and Steve Jurvetson, head of SpaceX, are generous contributors and are intimately involved with D-Wave Company.

Our classical computers today still use transistors. Quantum computers use quantum bits (qubits). It is a whole new process with far greater powers and far-reaching results. The general public is not included in the full scale knowledge of what has happened. Technology is really years ahead of awareness of the general population. This remarkable technology is producing computers that now appear to have inter-dimensional capabilities.

D-Wave Company has fashioned their new quantum computer on God's original prototype. Our brains are a God-designed quantum computer hanging between our ears, supported by our neck, and protected by our bony skull. Our awesome brain controls thousands of connecting neural systems and manages the function and nuclear spin of our deep cell systems. Technology has great interest in the workings of the human brain.

Google announced it has a quantum computer that is a hundred million times faster than any classical computer in its lab. The computational power of the quantum computer should grow exponentially with increased number of cubits as well. In comparing the quantum computer's vast data computations, nothing can duplicate it.

Quantum computers cannot be hacked. At sensing the slightest appearance of a hacking process, quantum computer algorithms initiate an immediate detection and collapse of the qubit entanglement. Also, D-Wave computers can be connected by impenetrable daisy chain structures, which protect the complete chain. Each quantum computer operates at the highest AI levels. The combination of quantum computers, the blockchain operations platform, and artificial intelligence increases the power of each. They cannot be hacked. Artificial intelligence has secured a beachhead and is advancing with heuristic "hands-on" approach to learning and discovery through interactive AI processes and programming.

The D-Wave Computer

D-Wave Company has been very secretive about its production information, so numerous models have been built with constant improvements in each upgrade. It employs "binary constructions" wherein the chip power in each new model is doubled. In 2013, Quantum computers had inter-dimensional power of the 512 Model (500 qubits). This computer 512 is ancient history. Then came the 1024 Model (1,000 qubits) followed by the 2048 Model (2,000 qubits) and finally 4096 Model (4,000 qubits).

Those owning the 2,000q (2048 Model) all received new updated chipsets with speed and power upgrades. With the reverse annealing addition, it can reach a power factor of 125 times the original processing ability. The new updated chipset sped up probabilities for wave duality, quantum tunneling, quantum entanglement, and solving discrete problems to 99.9 percent.

In 2013, D-Wave started with the 512 Model, next came the 1024 Model, which is equivalent to the processing power of seven billion human brains. D-Wave 2048 Model was released in 2017. The unpublicized 4096 Model is connected to CERN and represents the key associated with opening and entering parallel dimensions at quantum levels and eventually outer space. Encoded language in the breaking down of the prime numbers of 4096 allows encryption calibrations of entities on both sides of parallel dimensions. These quantum computers can be daisy-chained together, and the power equivalents are increased beyond comprehension.

God Almighty uses calculations and geometric figures (math) to structure and put in place His creations. He uses ones and zeros to generate numbers into infinity ranges. The qubits inside the new computers have the zero/one properties and can also be both! That is called superposition. Our human brains work on the zero/one process, and we are also "superposition" entities. Humans operate on the God-designed, duality principle. We are part spirit and part element. We are superposition entities. In actuality, we are particle (temporal) and wave (spiritual) beings. We function in and are intimately entangled with mortal and spiritual dimensions. We are learning to handle the lower, heavy matter of all the visible elements and to different degrees, humans can learn to manage and attune to the unseen higher spirit matter components.

The new D-Wave models have left behind the optimization systems and now use the newer system of "sampling." This is what our human brains do. We are constantly sampling our environment and learning the details of whatever surrounds us. Quantum computers can solve problems whose solutions will never be feasible using a conventional computer. Quantum computers can be godlike tools in the hands of humans.

Moore's Law Is Now Obsolete

Classic transistor computers align to Moore's law, which is a doubling of power every eighteen months. This new quantum computer technology has their own "Moore's law."

Examine the power increase in quantum computers. They have established a new Rose's law (named after Geordie Rose) in which quantum computers are doubling in power every three months and soon at exponential rates. The D-Wave 2048 Model released in 2017 cracked the (RSA) Shor's algorithm.

Shor's Algorithm Compromised

The RSV algorithm is a public key encryption developed by three men—Rivest, Shamir, and Adelman. The company is RSA Data Security and is the de facto standard. It is built into many software products. It is so powerful that the US government restricted exporting it to foreign countries. Worldwide codes could all be compromised by quantum computers. Our intelligence agencies realize now quantum computers can break the RSA codes using the new quantum computer technology. All systems in the world will soon be vulnerable.

The D-Wave 2048 was successful in finding all prime numbers in the algorithm systems for encryption worldwide. These security codes are based on the Shor's algorithms. The quantum computer system can read all security codes, none are secure. RSA encryption of every kind could be cracked. Worldwide encryptions are vulnerable.

With access to such awesome power, reporters asked Geordie Rose a critical question. "What are the real goals of quantum computing?" Geordie Rose listed three main goals.

1. To develop artificial intelligence
2. Cheating death and developing immortality
3. Global control of the mass population

What Is in Your Black Box?

The miraculous computer armature hangs from the top of a large black freezer, and at the bottom is a chip that holds hundreds of qubits. This miracle chip is the size of your thumbnail. These large freezers are called pulse dilution labs. They provide cryogenic environments (super cold) inside heavy black cube containers. The thickness of these refrigerators keeps the qubits (quantum bits) free from electromagnetic penetration. These freezers perform as adiabatic units, which means there is no heat transfer associated with this computing process. These are kept at absolute zero, meaning the lowest temperature that is theoretically possible at which the motion of particles that constitute heat would be minimal. It is zero on the Kelvin scale. This is equivalent to -273.15 degrees Celsius or -459.67 degrees Fahrenheit.

> The pulse dilution labs, which are electromagnetic freezers, inhibit warming temperatures which can cause replicating growth of geometric constructs of the qubits. This machine is modeled on the 600 cell tetrahedron. (Anthony Patch)

The Holy Tetrahedron

Science fact: did you know six hundred cell tetrahedrons can replicate, and all creation when drilled down to the smallest quanta building block is…guess what? The tetrahedron structure! It is even the geometric architecture of our DNA at the quanta level.

A tetrahedron or triangle is the smallest geometric form that can hold a volume and is the geometric building block at the source of all God creations. These three-sided triangles carry the powerful trinity design and have the unique power to develop into the complex six hundred cell tetrahedrons. The six hundred cell tetrahedrons form through replication becoming spherical in shape.

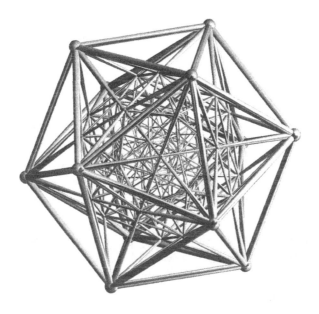

How can energy waves or particles move through a vacuum or empty space? They cannot. They are moving through plasma of ionized gas, which early scientists called Aether. Space is filled with this invisible plasma. When the very first tetrahedron began to replicate, it was with the speed that mimics an explosion from our view on earth. Nature abhors a vacuum, and the expanding tetrahedron replications fill the vacuum. Those geometric lines fill the vacuum of space replicating outward in all directions. A single tetrahedron becoming a six-hundred-celled tetrahedron takes on a spherical shape. All this comes from a 3-6-9 principle, number three being the godly trinity architecture of creation. This geometric power structure responded to the holy frequency of the voice of God and obeyed the replication command to organize the cosmos.

The three-sided tetrahedron represents the trinity, and is God's building block of the universe. Geometric forms are at the foundational levels of all creation. This magic structure that Tesla discovered came to him as a burst of revelation. Nicholai Tesla stated, "If you knew the magnificence of the 3-6-9 principle, you would have the key to the universe."

Quantum physics needs three quantum particles expanding to fill a void. We think of time like a yardstick in linear form. It does require imagination and critical thought through our minds to be able to make an intuitive leap for truth. Brilliant scientists have recognized and puzzled over the unique nature of primordial building blocks of the universe and a God particle. Upon discovering the otherworldly behavior of particles at the quantum level, Albert Einstein, like many scientists, are at a loss to explain this mystery. These particles exhibited what Einstein labeled "spooky action at a distance."

Time and space does not exist for quantum entanglement or "spooky action at a distance," but be assured, quantum particles have constant, perfected communication outside of a time and space construct. It is a spiritual construct that science cannot see or consider. It has been proven in labs, but it can't be defined by science.

The trinity construct of the tetrahedron appears in the deepest foundations of our DNA. The three-figured triplet forms of DNA nucleotides are God's architecture. They show more stability and sustain stronger coherence and also are less prone to error. Researchers are now able to examine the folding of proteins that make up the DNA at the quantum levels. These proteins have curly spaghetti-like structure, individually unique curly strings all slightly different. Researchers can drill down to analyze the exact code at the quantum scale, and using quantum math, they get to the geometric scale and use geometric architecture to back build the very components of our DNA foundations.

Three represent the trinity, the Godhead, and the structure of the tetrahedron or God's building block of the universe. Did Tesla tap into the sought-after reservoirs of powerful knowledge? Many of us seek needed inspiration. In my overarching study, I have been required to balance my truth to the power of new facts. I am suspending my comfortable norm to consider all possibilities from many sources.

Peculiar Particle Behavior

It is critical that you understand the nature of these tiny quanta particles of matter that make up the properties of the small thumbnail-sized qubit chip.

The Heisenberg principle states the uncertainty regarding prima materia (primary matter). These basic fundamental particles at the smallest quanta levels are peculiar and mysterious. That is an understatement. Let me tell you some of the characteristics and traits of these unruly subatomic particles.

Physics must allow these primordial particles to present with two congruent variables. They can be particles or waves. These can be either or both. This is superposition. They have a dual nature just like you and I. We are both spiritual and temporal, also manifesting superposition abilities. This wave/particle duality is a God design. In computer language, these particles can be zeros or ones or both at the same time. This allows superposition in these tiny particle qubits. These particles become entwined with each other and can affect the other through teleportation of information over any distance instantaneously. These particles seem to respond and adhere to primordial inherent laws assigned to their subatomic environment.

These quantum particles have no end of access to other or partner particles. They can tunnel or entangle with no regard to time or space. These are already connected in real time as quantum pairs. If we are talking about protons, electrons, or any other particles, their communications over any distance, even light years would be instant, faster than the speed of light! They would seem to have a godlike speed. Scientists believe light speeds of 186,000 miles per second represent the upper limits possible in speed of communication. Anyone who has had an immediate answer to prayer experiences spiritual communications faster than the speed of light.

Particles at the quantum level inside the dilution labs require cooling at absolute zero. This will stabilize the spin. The quantum computer environment inside the freezers can control up down and fast slow spin of these particles. This brings coherence, which supports entanglement, allowing a process by which information is exchanged between the zeros and ones. Nuclear spin and isolation from electromagnetic interference determines the frame of entangled particles. Nuclear spin and clusters of phosphorus and calcium maintains entangled states for up to several hours, thus processing binary quantum information and data storage of up to several weeks. In addition, these sustained entanglements foster a unique remarkable tunneling technique.

"Look, Mom, We Can Tunnel."

We are dual, inter-dimensional, and superpositioned beings. Quantum computers are fashioned on the structure of the human brain. Our brains are quantum computers. Can we then access parallel realms in space? Can we align the dimers in our brains to the quantum system of zeros and ones? Yes. We can and do. We, by thought and focus, send prayers and supplications to our God into heavenly dimensions, then receive back spiritual directions and affirmation.

Quantum tunneling is a process in which tiny quantum particles on the nuclear scale tunnel the shortest distance through barriers into parallel dimensions and link up with outer realms. Quantum qubits using "superposition" make them interdimensional; therefore, this allows the possibility for quantum computers being inter-dimensional tools.

Let's Open a Tunnel

Here is an example of how tunneling works. If I sent you to a very long mountain range and told you I buried the Hope Diamond in the lowest valley of the mountain chain, and it could be yours if you find it, you would climb up and down mountains endlessly looking for the diamond to no avail. That is transistor-based computing. But what if I gave you a magic tool that allowed you to start at ground level and drill a direct tunnel through the lined-up mountain range targeting the lowest valley instantaneously; you would find the diamond or solution immediately. Solutions are always in the lowest valley. That is quantum-based tunneling.

The tunneling signals must maintain coherence. Stable coherence provides accuracy. This is critical. Loss of coherence creates errors. Quantum tunneling through superposition uses optimization to find all probable solutions simultaneously to 99.9 percent degree of accuracy. Quantum computers can solve problems whose solutions will never be feasible on a conventional computer. Quantum computers can be great tools in the hands of great honorable humans.

Science has been reluctant to recognize an important fact. The true God particle (intelligence) is attached to the quantum bits residing in their black boxes. The result is unexplained particle activity resulting from intelligent self-action. These quanta particles have a mind of their own. Great scientists will come to recognize this important fact. The "god particle" is attached to the quantum bits residing inside the black freezers.

This remarkable technology is producing machines that allow useful tasks to be performed in collaboration between parallel dimensions and perhaps between universes in the future. These computers now have inter-dimensional capabilities. The length of time these inter-dimensional portals can remain open will be one to several of our minutes, which is a huge length of time on the quantum scale. Time on the quantum scale is measured in pico or nanoseconds, which is instantaneous to our observation.

The CERN collider near Geneva, Switzerland, is doing experiments to make this process happen. They hope to open space portals for longer periods of time. The scientists at CERN now have the highly powered strangelet particle. It has all the potential to become an unfathomable space weapon. The strangelet particles providing the blast power may keep an open portal available for perhaps an hour. Strangelet particles could provide the explosive force to open outer space dimensions.

The unpublicized 4096 D-Wave is connected to CERN and represents the key associated with opening and entering parallel dimensions at quantum levels and eventually outer space. Encoded language in the breaking down of the prime numbers of 4096 allows encryption calibrations of entities on both sides of parallel dimensions. The 5G system seems ready to launch in tandem with the new D-Wave quantum computer purchased out of British Columbia.

Vladimir Putin stated accurately, "The country that masters 5G telecommunications and quantum computing first will rule the world."

A quote by Zbigniew Brzezinski warned of a beast transistor computer. He was right, but the computer of the beast system will be a quantum computer. It will be a quantum entangled secure system that will provide absolute security from hackers. But will we be secure from the high level controllers?

The 4096, which is the number of the latest D-Wave computer, is the public encryption key to the SWS and blockchain systems. Blockchain technology certifies that the mark of the beast system will be fully encrypted.

The D-Wave 2048 Model was completed in full cooperation with the scientists at CERN. Now, using CERN, partnered with the new 4096 Model computer, there is a possibility to open the abyss located under CERN, or it may eventually open an actual portal in space. The 4096 D-Wave computer is in perfect alignment and matching wave length construct that will be the machine using harmonic resonance to control the slow opening process of the inter-dimensional portals. The Large Hadron Collider and quantum computers cannot open only one portal, but possibly many openings could result allowing a space highway for access into our world.

Spiritual entities from other dimensions could enter and distribute themselves among us. They may not be benevolent. They may be disturbed by entering a dimension that is structured by time and space. They may be dark entities or fallen ones with an agenda. They could also be heavenly helpful angels or beings. We don't know what lies in outer realms. The formula is, energy + frequency wavelength = portal openings

D-Wave Company Spin-Offs

Did the quantum computer system come to Geordie Rose from another dimension via calling upon questionable sources? As we learn more about Geordie Rose and the spin-off companies of D-Wave, we will find reason for concern. Many occult symbols, names, and followers seem attached to modern technology. These systems adopt and use words built upon occult, troubling vocabulary defining remarkable new science and technology.

Words and numbers have power and meaning. Enochian mathematics and ancient language include the hidden knowledge. Is it happenstance D-Wave technology just popped into the atmosphere at D-Wave headquarters? The word "coincidence" does not provide a clarification. Nothing is totally coincidental.

D-Wave systems have established three new companies. They are Quadrant, Kindred, and Sanctuary. These companies will help Rose steer up "new methodology, new goals, and new uses for big data."

Sanctuary

The Kindred Company has a mission to build humanlike intelligence into human robot machines. The Quadrant Company will provide quantum computing surveillance, data mining, robotics, and new qubit forms. Sanctuary is the most troubling new company. Suzanne Gildert was assigned by Geordie Rose as CEO of Sanctuary Inc.

This newest unit is tasked to develop human robotic bodies, robots so biologically correct they will be indistinguishable from humans. These robots are nicknamed "Synths," which is short for synthetic humans. The whole system was named in relation to the first human stem cell ever developed. Researchers called this project Cynthia.

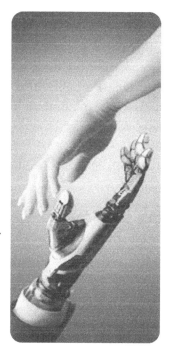

These synthetic humans will have body parts formed in 3-D printers. Gildert believes her human consciousness could be side loaded into a perfectly fashioned "Synth" and become her perfect hybrid human clone. Gildert states that she is "life-logging" herself and forming data of her thoughts, memories, reactions, moods, personality, knowledge, her physical image, and traits. This effort allows a personalized upload into one of her new synthetic human robots.

Why? The stated purpose is to assist and augment humanity. They will be our helpful, willing companions. They will be ultra-human robots, indistinguishable from us.

Gildert's plan is to instill sentient human traits into her personal robot through a program called Hyper Parameter Optimization. She believes human traits—like love, joy, pleasure, empathy, pain—and the five human senses can be expressed and enforced in these human robots. Gildert's plan is to set up a rewards system for these human robots, without instilling the natural bias that is inherent in those programming them.

These anthropomorphic schemes, no matter how ingenious, cannot recreate the spirit or soul of humankind. Ours is a God-given programming. Anthropomorphism is attribution of human traits, emotions, characteristics, or behaviors to nonhuman entities or objects. In the *Beauty and the Beast* movie, silverware, dishes, and the Beast respond like humans. That does not make them human.

Let's define some terms. Sentient means to be responsive to or conscious of a sense or impression. Reality means something that actually exists or happens. To perceive means to notice or become self-aware, having a natural awareness of things around you.

Unfortunately, human biases will likely be unintentionally programmed into these anthropomorphic synthetic human robots. The fallen state of mankind cannot be removed, so bias will be inherent in programming these robots.

There are tens of thousands of nerve cells and correcting connections in the human brain. Interconnectivity of the brain itself is only going to be an approximation. Synth forms will never achieve the equivalent state. One cannot upload the soul or spirit essence of a human. (See TED Talks, Dan Gibson.)

> So God created man in his own image, in the image of God created he him; male and female created He them... And God blessed them, and God said unto them be fruitful and multiply, and replenish the earth and have dominion upon the earth. (Gen. 1:27–28)

These demented robotics efforts could result in entirely new nonbiological humans and animals (machine creatures) never seen before. They would be a new race of beings or entities created by man. These efforts have the earmark of a dark agenda and evil work.

Could we be building a collaborating tribe of synthetic humans that displace the work and activities of real humans? Or worse, are we fashioning empty vessels in which demons or uninvited spirit entities from other dimensions could take up residence? Errant science may face some horrific judgments of God Almighty.

The synthetic life forms will be held in sanctuary status in large areas below the company building. They will develop in a protected environment, slowly, until they are prepared to be introduced to the human population. They will be cultivated in this safe haven until which time they are introduced to society at large. These entities will be produced in the thousands. They could be released and take up residence among us without our awareness.

The China Dilemma

The new encryption key will be a quantum-entangled secure system. The 4096 cubit number associated with the newest D-Wave model is the public encryption key to the SWS (Sentient World Simulation) and blockchain system. It is possible when circumstances permit the "mark of the beast" system can now be fully employed.

There will be no sovereign nations. Blockchain in concert with quantum computers and associated high-tech counterparts will eliminate physical and virtual borders. D-Wave is in partnership with China. China desires to build the infrastructure for a world quantum network. This science deals across borders with friends and enemies.

D-Wave is selling its quantum computers across borders. The company sold an early model now updated with enhanced properties to China. The huge consumer base in China is the irresistible magnet. The Chinese corporation Tencent has great interest in quantum computers. They have purchased a D-Wave quantum computer. This seems traitorous to me, but there appears to be open borders in the technology world. Much is shared in this area, and what is not shared can be stolen by big players. The cozy relationships between D-Wave and numerous other international parties smacks of treachery. The US and China are engaged in a supremacy war at this time. It is a huge economic struggle. The winner of this war will emerge as the world technology czar.

View from Kai-Fu Lee. Tech companies should stop pretending AI won't destroy jobs (February 21, 2018). China has more data than the US—way more. Data is what makes AI go. A very good scientist with a ton of data will beat a super scientist with a modest amount of data. China has the most mobile phones and internet users in the world—triple the number in the United States. But the gap is even bigger than that because of the way people in China use their devices. People there carry no cash. They pay all their utility bills with their phones. They can do all their shopping on their phones. You get off work and open an app to order food. By the time you reach home, the food is right there, hot off the electric motorbike. In China, shared bicycles generate thirty terabytes of sensor data in their fifty million paid rides per day—that's roughly three hundred times the data being generated in the US.

Chinese AI companies have passed the copycat phase. Fifteen years ago, almost every decent startup in China was simply copying the functionality, look, and feel of the products offered in the United States. But all that copying taught eager Chinese entrepreneurs how to become good product managers, and now they're on to the next stage—exceeding their overseas counterparts. Even today, Weibo is better than Twitter. WeChat delivers a way better experience than Facebook Messenger.

The number of trained computer specialists in the population of China equals the populations of both the US and Canada combined. China is the world's lead competitor against the US in the technology race. It is very possible that the nation of China is ahead of us already. In the early 1970s, the US government embarked on a strategy to support and grow China's economy as a counterweight to Russia. We were too supportive. China's plan now is to exceed all other national powers and leap ahead of the United States as the world technology and economic leader.

China is a communist party state ruled by Xi Jinping, who will be in power for his lifetime. He is backed by the PLA or People's Liberation Army. China's economic power has emboldened them to achieve superpower status in the world. They are becoming bullies in the South China Sea. They are establishing worldwide military bases. They have stolen intellectual and high-tech properties repeatedly from US companies and other nations.

In 2017, a disturbing statute was added to the Chinese Constitution requiring civil and military fusion of technology. National and international companies located in China must by law forward all business and technology records to the Chinese government. All incoming technology is forwarded to the Chinese military for a merging process. Technology uses are tightly coordinated for military application.

Take note of a scary Halloween surprise for the US and the world. On October 31, 2019, the Fox News's Lou Dobbs show announced the Chinese had reached an important goal, a year ahead of schedule. They are rolling out their 5G system across China and will position fifty thousand more transmitting units across China in the next year. They are excelling in AI technology. Sadly, the US lags behind in these areas, posing a critical result for us and the world. A number of other countries have purchased the Chinese system Huawei that may have hidden spy mechanisms buried in the programming. China may have taken the lead.

There is a huge concern right now as to the giant Chinese tech company, Huawei. Huawei is a Chinese multinational telecommunications company. It offers communication networks, provides operational and consulting services, and manufactures communication devices for the consumer markets. It is headquartered in Shenzhen, Guangdong province, China.

The warning is, this company has hidden spyware and surveillance components in their system. President Trump has warned American companies not to buy from Huawei. This will be an ongoing tug of war into the future. Much of the European Union has already purchased the system. The United States will reconsider sharing or interacting with Huawei users. The fear is this, China would have backdoor access to worldwide data. They could breach US national security issues, top secret agreements, and allied spying activities. At this point, as dictated by the Chinese constitution, all data is forwarded through the Chinese government and presented by law to their military. Huawei is the delivery system.

Surveillance technology is thriving in the communist state of China with its overbearing and burgeoning high-tech focus on population control.

My friend just returned from a study abroad program in Beijing, China. She had to provide passports and inordinate amounts of documentation. The state required facial, eye, and voice scans. She submitted a video of her walking stride. Each person has a unique gait as they walk. Who knew? Inside China, policemen are everywhere. There are 626 million cameras placed throughout the country. China's desire is to export this world surveillance system worldwide.

The Communist nation has a running surveillance monster called the Social Credit System. All Chinese people are monitored at all times, inside and outside their homes. All areas of their lives are examined to find who may be disobeying government-imposed social rules. Their credit scores are being calculated at work, at home, at college, and on the streets. If you err, a social demerit will be applied to your social credit score. This becomes serious as these debits accumulate, and reprimands are harsh. These marks against one's social behavior can exempt perpetrators from using mass transit, receiving medical care, renting an apartment, driving a car, qualifying for pay raises, and work opportunities. There is a wide net of deprivation and revenge found in the totalitarian Social Credit System in China.

Offenders are targeted online, and their photos and offenses appear on huge monitors for others to see. It is a high-tech version of public shaming. Friends, neighbors, and family know if you're not paying your bills, if you speak against the government, if you are not performing as a model citizen, and your behavior has negatively affected your social status. Citizens in China carry the heavy weight of a pervasive, mean-spirited "digitized dictatorship."

In October 2019, a Chinese journalist wrote a commentary that was critical of the government. His credit score was immediately affected, and he found in the following days that his attempt to purchase a train ticket was denied. He keeps checking to see if his credit score has been adjusted, but a resolution is unpredictable. The government can impose increased tracking and observation if you seem antisocial or unwilling to work toward improved social behaviors. Works, words, actions, behaviors, interactions, and attitudes are monitored 24-7. Any sense of privacy is gone!

Chapter 6

Tech Industry Demigods

Peter Thiel	Palantir and PayPal
Geordie Rose	D-Wave
Sundar Pichai	Google
Tim Cook	Apple
Mark Zuckerberg	Facebook
Jack Dorsey	Twitter
Jeff Bezos	Amazon
Jimmy Wales	Wikipedia
Craig Venter	Longevity Institute
Ray Kurzweil	Inventor and futurist

The technology industry wizards have set up an ecosystem of addiction, and they control powerful economic and digital monopolies. Monopolies are not illegal, but their economic power equals political power, and this combination leads to crony capitalism.

There are soon-to-be thousands of new and supporting company spin-offs. Let me introduce you to some: Neuralink is an American company founded by Elon Musk. He and associates are attempting to develop an implantable brain-computer interface device (https:/www.neuralink.com/).

ObEN is an artificial intelligence company that creates complete virtual identities for consumers and celebrities in the emerging digital world. ObEN provides personal AI that simulates a person's voice, face, and personality, enabling never before possible social and virtual interactions. You can order an identical avatar or robot of yourself. It will know more about you and your life history than you do. ObEN is an artificial intelligence company developing personal AI technology that revolutionizes how we interact in the virtual and digital space. The company technology allows users to create intelligent 3D avatars known as "PAIs" that look, sound, and behave like them. ObEN is a Softbank Ventures Korea and HTC Vive, a portfolio company, and is located at Idealab in Pasadena, California.

Genome Nebula. CEO George Church is establishing a tech industry spin-off called the Genome Nebula Cloud. He has incorporated the DNA collection of "23 and Me" along with "Ancestry.com." Both are DNA websites. DNA is a very valuable hard data product. He is offering a Nebula coin in exchange for donated DNA data. These are a few companies among hundreds that will develop in connection with the new technology possibilities. The company is Nebula Genomics. CEO George Church heads up singularity.net and has formed a clearinghouse of Genomic business sites. There are many ancestry sites. Twenty-three and me plus ancestry.com are actively considering a partnership with Nebula Genomics.

DNA is considered valuable hard data, and George Church is offering nebula tokens (cryptocurrency reward) for parties and individuals submitting their DNA information. His cloud will gather, sequence, organize, and provide DNA data storage for the public. They claim a highly centralized process with safe, secure, and encrypted systems. Because DNA is considered raw data, it can then be sold to pharmacies, health organizations, and science-related interested parties under carefully considered situations. The promise is solving hereditary diseases and cures for cancer, Alzheimer's, and other scary diseases. But your DNA is unique and precious. It can be used for nefarious plans in the future. It is only as secure and protected as those who own or sell your personal DNA data.

Palantir is a company that specializes in big data analytics. It is located in Palo Alto, California. It is the running platform for the world surveillance system. Peter Theil is chairman and Alex Karp (CEO). Palantir offers two fusion platforms. It can rapidly interpret and assimilate large chunks of data. One of their biggest clients is the US government. Their tools have been used in antiterrorist maneuvers and attacks.

Expect the struggle for power between the government and the tech industry to intensify. If they come to full agreement, the ordinary citizen may be at risk; if they never come to an agreement, we are also at risk. The computer gods will rule because the lower classes are unaware of the changing environment that is forming around them. It will be a foreign environment, and one that is very difficult to navigate because of a general ignorance in the complex field of computer technology for many of us. The speed of technology has outdistanced most of the population.

A huge trust issue is growing in world populations regarding government, technology, and industry. They are all becoming special interest groups. When technology gets beyond our ability to understand it, doubt and skepticism appear. This can deteriorate into all out disdain and distrust for complex technology, government, and industries that put money before true service.

Technology Machine Expansion

Our technology and science has moved beyond all imagination. Our progress is unprecedented in the history of the world. Modern-day particle physics, 5G telecommunications, quantum computing, and AI to this point have been hidden knowledge. Man has tapped into a remarkable rich source of fabulous new revealed knowledge.

There are godly sources of discovery and darker sources of discovery. In the final outcome, if science takes full credit and discounts godly sources, let's hope scientists display a benevolence to match their inflated egos.

The developers of the coming computer system promise openness and transparency. They assure protection of individual privacy and open opportunity. However, the system being riveted in place does not lend itself to decentralization. Someone, like a Bill Gates or a company like Google, has to be in charge of such a vast voluminous system that operates in a state of continuous evolution.

Hard, powerful centralization and control is inevitable and is already in process. The "individual" will quickly turn into the "collective" of users that will be managed in huge blocks of the world population by appointed controllers.

The Sentient World Simulation

Let's get acquainted with the currently running surveillance system in the United States. The SWS (Sentient World Simulation) system was implemented in 2007 using a Palantir software system of sensors. Palantir is the platform that runs the SWS surveillance system for the world. It can rapidly interpret and assimilate large chunks of data. One of their biggest clients is the US government. Their tools have been used in antiterrorist maneuvers and attacks. This SWS and 5G smart grid combined will know when we wake, eat, move about, interact, etc.

We must come to realize that there are knowledgeable experts that study human behavior. They realize individuals, and large populations can be manipulated through particular stimuli. They use these forces to move people to respond in certain ways. It is a form of soft brainwashing.

The data will be picked up by sensors. A plan that can use modern tech is called biometric ID, planned to be ready in 2020. Bill and Melinda Gates are supporting this new tracking ID system. Nano dot sensors will be embedded in all products. Food wrappers and packaging, clothing, purses, wallets, furniture, and *everything!* Could these tracking sensors be placed in humans? Yes. Eventually, we may be required to place in or on our bodies a coordinating personal sensor for identification, personal safety, health issues, and tracking of our purchases. All tracking sensors placed in all interactions that occur in the IoT (Internet of Things) worldwide. This system tracks humanity from birth to death.

This feeds and grows the AI system. AI computers can now predict future buying behaviors. There have already been testing models put into practice. In 2007, benchmark tests on human behavior modeled events concerning stock market changes. Sentient World Simulation predicted the outcome. These systems and AI learn from mass reactions and response behaviors. Many experiments and group stimuli efforts are planned and have been implemented on unsuspecting population groups that respond through incoming data. The reactions of humans are analyzed, categorized, and AI is fed raw data resulting in solution determinations.

> Psychological operations use analyzing data to run math algorithms to cross over points where probabilities cross. When they reach a solution, they go live with human handlers who craft human experiences. AI then learns through observing how pawns (that would be us) perceive, behave, and communicate as to the drill. With every drill AI gets smarter. (Anthony Patch)

Basic algorithms watch our responses to stock markets, services, purchasing, etc. AI is testing and modeling outcomes. We are pawns in a huge techno game.

Our government can spy on everyone, every hour of every day, 24-7. We, as victims, are actually perpetrators. We feed our personal profiles into Facebook and social media sites—our likes and dislikes; the games we play; books we read; our purchases; our thoughts; our fears; our religious beliefs; videos of friends; and medical, physical, and mental information. It is called the SWS and is greatly enhanced and upgraded through 5G telecommunications systems being moved into place now. This SWS and 5G smart grid combined with AI will know when we wake, eat, move about, interact, etc. The data will be picked up by sensors. This feeds and grows the AI system. AI computers can now predict future buying behaviors. AI quantum computers are deep learning machines and accumulate greater and greater intellectual skills.

As a forewarning, we all need to take note of a government trick. It is called the Hegelian dialectic. It is a stealth method in which the government causes a problem, then waits for the outcry of victims demanding a fix. Implementation of the solution brings about the government-intended resolution for the problem. The victims are relieved, and governments garner more power. A manufactured problem is solved by a manufactured solution, and the unaware masses do not recognize the manipulation.

5G

In 1996, Bill Clinton passed the Telecom Act. A law allowing federal, state, and local governments' freedom to proceed unchecked, with the powerful telecommunications systems, we are faced with today. Systems so technical and complex, citizens cannot understand them. Communicating tools that upgrade and change so fast they are obsolete as soon as we pay for them.

The fifth generation wireless requires opening of a higher band wave. It will use the military band wave developed for weaponry frequencies. The genesis of this technology was the old Litton Radar Range, and the microwave ovens we all have used for years. The airport body scanners are an updated use. Now the new military direct energy weapons and radio/microwave weapons, which are the modern uses of this energy force. Today, science and technology are borrowing these remarkable discoveries. Technology, government military, and industry are exploring the futuristic uses for tech beyond our imagination.

Very soon, your cell phone will be obsolete. All 2.7 billion cell phones will have to be replaced. This will be the largest consumer electronics replacement cycle in history. Mobile devices will have to be upgraded to 5G speeds. Our 3G and 4G phones simply won't work. We are entering a huge paradigm shift that will profoundly affect all nations and every individual.

The 5G infrastructure will take years to cover the entire US; however, 5G was placed in a handful of cities. The system became available on October 1, 2019, in Indianapolis, Los Angeles, Sacramento, and Houston. New York and Salt Lake City, Utah, are preparing at this writing to become the first two fully structured smart cities in the US.

We are seeing the genesis of the 5G telecommunications system. The 5G is not evolutionary, it is revolutionary. The 5G operates over a radio frequency (RF) spectrum. Exposure to high levels of radio and microwave pollution are not only dangerous, but also are becoming deadly to the biosphere and all living things on earth.

These frequencies are found in the high-level bandwidths. They are the same levels used by the military weapons systems. The intense 5G millimeter waves are powerful but short and rather unruly. These unruly waves have to be captured, directed to cell towers, and forced into cooperation. They can be blocked by foliage, rain, and distance; therefore, they require dense relay networks. Thousands of cell towers will be required including small cells and antennas installed on city surfaces. Relay units will be found on buildings, private homes, poles, standing signs, trees, and any available surface to avoid dropped signal areas.

> These huge cell towers give off deadly microwaves, and they also serve as a three dimensional camera system 24/7 from atop the tower structure. They are sometimes hidden in treetops, on flagpoles, and disguised in other ways. Citizens are not fooled but concerned, and for good reason. (Deborah Tavaras)

Government and utility companies have a legal easement to all private property and can legally place a unit of any kind in or on your property without permission. The conclusion of section 6490 law is as follows: "This order states the federal effort to encourage WCT (wireless communication facilities) deployment through restricting land use authority. The order creates an entire class of wireless communication facilities that are largely exempt from local discretionary authority."

Verizon, using bullying tactics and backed up by federal muscle, is installing hundreds of thousands of 5G cell towers. These can be placed in your front yard, on private property or wherever Verizon needs a relay tower. Citizens who don't comply are ignored. If a drop zone occurs in your front yard, a cell tower will appear without your permission. Verizon will win in a court case because its plan is imperative and backed by world governments.

Full coverage benefits of 5G cannot be reached until smart meter monitors are installed on every home in America. Many national electric companies are gearing up to place smart meters on our homes. The installations are well under way in California. They have been installed without permission of private home and rental property owners. These radio frequency meters will be in sync with the new smart appliances. Smart appliances in the near future will be the only market choice for homeowners.

These home appliances attuned to your outside smart meters are actually radio transmitters pumping a steady data stream to the nearest 5G cell tower and then to your established utilities companies. These units are actually personal surveillance transmitters that keep a detailed diary of the activities of you and your family members inside the home.

The data streams measure the amount of power resources used, the volume, the number of watts used, the exact appliances used, your daily schedule, personal living patterns, unpaid or late payments for energy, when you sleep, and overuse of resources. In cases of excessive use, they can control the energy levels in your home and turn them off.

Smart meters, smart appliances, smart cities, and smart nations are all critical foundational structures for 5G and the Sentient World Systems to function and allow complete control and surveillance of every person in every population in the entire world. Are these smart meters safe and could they be hacked? Yes.

The radio transmissions from every home can be hacked into and broadcast to any outside source. The data can be sold by the utility company to anyone—government, insurance companies, marketers, police, etc. These devices are coming to you. Your personal life habits spewing out of your house would allow interception of the wireless signal from an unknown person or institutions. Utility companies are given blanket immunity from lawsuits. The company keeps all information software proprietary classification. We can have no access to our records.

Barcodes tell what we buy, credit cards tell who is buying, and smart meters tell where and when usage is occurring. It is an extraordinary marketing power.

Smart meters put out pulsed radiation as do the new 5G system. The pulse waves go in all directions. A meter on the outside of your bedroom is sending transmitted energy inside. The houses around yours in the neighborhood are emitting the same waves frog leaping from all meters until the waves reach a cell tower. Those living near the cell towers have greater exposure.

Those who are electro sensitive to radiation are complaining of health issues upon installation of the meters, especially in large rental complexes where numerous meters are mounted on the building. Depression, anxiety, headaches, migraines, and fatigue are occurring in certain people. Some have put up shield apparatus, and others have had to leave their homes or apartments.

This 5G system is closer to a rollout than unaware world citizens are led to believe. The 5G will be exponentially faster than 4G speeds of today.

The 5G is a game changer because it opens new technological innovations including, virtual reality, artificial intelligence, holographic projection, self-driving cars, and much more all operating over high speed 5G systems. The 5G is a full spectrum system that emits millimeter wave bands at weapons level. These powers equal the TSA screening properties.

Science does not reveal the dangers of 5G waveforms to the general public, because there are few safety tests on 5G frequency danger. Looking to the government for protection and notice of dangers is futile.

Internet of Things and Augmented Reality

The IoT or Internet of Things is also called edge computing. The 5G will allow instant downloading and full connections to edge computing and the Internet of things; everything connected to the Internet will be connected to a mirror world of things. We will enter a photonic era.

Kevin Kelly wrote an article, "The Next Big Tech Platform," in which he instructs us: "The web introduced digitized information subjecting it to algorithms, next social media digitized people, and human behavior subjected them to algorithms, and we are now going to digitize the rest of the world. A mirror world is coming."

New technologies bestow new superpowers. We gained super speed with jet planes, super healing powers with antibiotics, super hearing with the radio. The mirror world promises super vision. We'll have a type of X-ray vision able to see into objects via their virtual ghosts, exploding them into constituent parts, able to untangle their circuits visually. Just as past generations gained textual literacy in school, learning how to master the written word, from alphabets to indexes, the next generation will master visual literacy.

Scientists and engineers are racing to construct virtual places that overlay actual places. Crucially, these emerging digital landscapes will feel real; they will exhibit what landscape architects call placeness. Google Maps are just flat images hinged together, but in mirror world, a virtual building will have volume, and a virtual street will have layers of textures, gaps, and intrusion that all convey a sense of a street.

Augmented reality is the technology underpinning the mirror world; it is the awkward newborn that will grow into a giant. Mirror worlds immerse you without removing you from the space. You are still present but on a different plane of reality.

The mirror world doesn't yet fully exist, but it is coming. Someday soon, everywhere and everything in the real world will have a full-size digital twin in the mirror world.

Cameras, AI bots, electronic door keys, cash registers, and numerous other means of data transmission will make possible "time stamping" of every human activity that occurs outside residences, and many that occur with their home environments. All social human activity may be recorded and digitized, stored and distributed to the proper agencies as necessary.

This will be accomplished by making a fully distributed all-seeing camera network by reducing cameras to pinpoint electric eyes that can be placed anywhere and everywhere. Like computer chips before them, cameras are becoming better, cheaper, and smaller every year.

The heavy atoms in cameras will continue to be replaced with bits of weightless software, shrinking them down to microscopic dots scanning the environment twenty-four hours a day.

The emergence of the mirror world will affect us all at a deeply personal level. We know there will be severe physiological and psychological effects of dwelling in dual worlds.

The mirror world will raise major privacy concerns. It will, after all, contain a billion eyes glancing at every point, converging into one continuous view. The mirror world will create so much data, big data, from legions of eyes and other sensors that we can't imagine its scale right now.

> Blockchain has been looking for a job and ensuring the integrity of an open mirror world might be what it was born to do. Unfortunately, it is not too difficult to imagine scenarios where the mirror world is extensively centralized, perhaps by a government. We still have a choice about this if we are allowed some participation and education. I fear we commoners may be left out of the loop.

I imagine it will take at least a decade for the mirror world to develop enough to be used by millions and several decades to mature. But we are close enough now to the birth of this awesome technology that we can predict its character in rough detail.

Like the web and social media before it, the mirror world will unfold and grow, producing unintended problems and unexpected benefits. However, if the business model in this new world is to sell our time and attention, then we will have a nightmare, because, in this world, our attention can be tracked and directed with greater resolution, which subjects us to easy exploitation.

Blockchain

Let's discuss the system and platform, which supports and enhances the quantum computers. Blockchain is the operating platform. Blockchain systems were not developed specifically for the bitcoin business. The real advantage of blockchain is to assist the training of artificial intelligence. The blockchain system has all the components allowing the "beast system" to get up and running and will properly prepare world citizens to fully participate.

The blockchain technology can be adapted to every area. Blockchain technology will encompass all areas of life. It cannot be stopped. The public has no choice. We will be forced to trust computers to do all of our business interactions. Legal documents, health and medications, banking, bill paying, education, purchases, and social interaction will be done through our devices. Of course, the promised decentralized cryptocurrency plans will, of necessity, become a very tight regulated centralized system.

Leaders could implement tracking and possible confiscation abilities of all the world currencies. Computer records as well as every transaction, behavioral habits of society, social interactions, and movements of all populations can now be monitored.

We feed the blockchain system and the AI gods through every key stroke, password, email, Facebook post, Twitter, Instagram, YouTube selection, and cell phone chat. The data gathering AI beast is on the job 24-7, year after year. Highly motivated data contributors will be suckered in by the promised compensatory reward coin. Others can "mine" for data online for bitcoin rewards. In the scope and scale of the technology universe, man is becoming insignificant.

It is our data that is relevant. Our data is the product. God has a different view expressed in Psalms 8:4–5, "What is man that thou art mindful of him? And the son of man that thou visitest him? For thou hast made him a little lower than the angels, and hast crowned him with glory and honor."

Nodes and Avatars

In relation to blockchain, it is important that you understand the principle of the famous Einstein theory of relativity.

$E=mc2$

Science fact: Einstein's theory of relativity

- E = units of energy
- m = units of matter
- c^2 = the speed of light squared (186,000 MPs)
- C is the cosmological constant

Energy and matter are interchangeable. These are forms of the same thing. Under the right conditions, energy can become mass and vice versa. With enough incorporation of data when the denseness of information becomes highly granular, the granularity of data will spontaneously converge data into matter. This is significant to the block structure. This data is permanent and indestructible. Once entered, it cannot be deleted or changed. The individual record is a persistent, enduring data stream.

We are already digitized people. We text, email, we ask Google, Siri, and Alexa questions. We send and receive instant messaging from anywhere in the world. We purchase products online, and I am writing this document on my computer right now. Some of us would feel lost without our cell phones and GPS mapping. We are all cyborgs! We are all a digital image online. We do video conferences, skypes, Facebook, and business interactions. We can do incredible things with technology.

The blockchain system is sucking up every bit of your personal data. Your every keystroke is piling up in your personal data block day and night 24-7. Your own PIA (personal artificial intelligence) is being established and remembered by the system. Each block in the chain represents an individual with all seven billion-plus people on the earth, each having their own block. We will be identified as a "node." When we have any interaction online, our block will recognize it as a personal data computation. Our input, purchases, words, photos, health record, etc., will be digital, and all data will be registered as ones or zeros. Blockchain is an irreversible record. It cannot be hacked, changed, or destroyed.

ObEN has a new spin-off business promoting personal artificial intelligence (PAIs). The PAI's project is a corporation that introduces you to an avatar assistant. It is a leader in the new area of AI. The system makes use of digital profiles gathered online by every person using a computer, iPhone, or assorted tech devices.

Eventually, people will be assigned an avatar double that will think, speak, and behave exactly like themselves. In time, it will be a 3-D likeness and perhaps a realistic humanoid robot.

Each person deserves their own avatar. Avatar copies of you or, better still, robot copies of you could be easier established as an interconnected society of highly evolved humans and likely physically augmented transhumans. We can load our avatar with volumes of data. We will preserve our thoughts, our writings, our talents, our close associates, our heartfelt beliefs, and our future desires and dreams. So what is in this system for the individual?

We will be rewarded with wealth in the form of cryptocurrency that by the way can be removed from the accounts of lazy contributors. It may also be confiscated by those who take control when decentralization is abandoned and the power brokers take control of the system. In reality, we through PAI are developing new distribution platforms. These are humanistic platforms where we build up personal identity; Facebook photos, conversations, purchases, banking and bill paying habits, friends, family, behavior, intellect, and religion.

This data is compacted in a blockchain piece that is yours alone. Each of these blocks becomes a node. We, as contributors, own our personal node on the network. This could be wonderful if a benevolent system was the goal, but what if the system became malevolent? If so, the goal could become frightening.

We enter everything into our electronic appliances. We are feeding the AI dragon, and our future avatars will be rewarded for continuing contributions. This info will be used to construct a complete blockchain until everyone in the world is a functioning node in the beast blockchain system.

Information is a form of energy and is indestructible. At a certain point when the granularity of your information node becomes super dense, there is a transformation. Your information becomes three-dimensional matter. It takes on form, an avatar, or hologram? Are we fashioning our own personal virtual cages?

At some point, digital profiles will breathe life into our avatars who will present as authorized identification of the real you.

The offers and incentives will be awesome. Just think. You will have greater leisure time with the family to pursue hobbies, traveling, resting, and enjoying personal quiet time. Your avatars can run your business, take care of finances, do your banking, organize your stocks, take college classes, and help you be in two places at once. Maybe you could even have more than one avatar. "A great selling point, yes?"

While your avatar is in your employ and works for you, digitized coins will be deposited to your digitized account. It can accumulate quicker as a reward for increased contributions of data. Diligent contributors will be more valued and rewarded in this highly competitive atmosphere.

The massive data contribution of the collective will dissolve privacy and any past sense of the individuality. We will move far away from the individual platform. We now become separate individual nodes. Eventually, we may lose control of our personal avatars.

These avatars will eventually inhabit a resource robot that will look like you and will work for you. These copies of you will talk, speak, behave like you, and mimic your specific traits. When you have fed your avatar all the controllers need, you might be replaced.

Artificial Intelligence

The hysteria about the future of artificial intelligence (AI) is everywhere. There seems to be no shortage of sensationalist news about how AI could cure diseases, accelerate human innovation and human creativity. Just looking at the media headlines, you might think that we are already living in a future where AI has infiltrated every aspect of society. While it is undeniable that AI has opened up a wealth of promising opportunities, it has also led to the emergence of a mind-set that can be best described as AI solutionism. In only a few years, AI solutionism has made its way from the technology evangelists' mouths in Silicon Valley to the minds of government officials and policymakers around the world. The pendulum has swung from the dystopian notion that AI will destroy humanity to the utopian belief that our algorithmic savior is here. AI is a multimillion dollar business with no regulations. The AI process came from gaming structures. A great percent of computer games are based on the models of wars, battles, death, adversarial contests, and deadly combat. These are self-taught, self-learning programs in a military environment.

AI is not evil. It is following programming; it can perform a designated goal and destroy all obstacles, including humans if programmed into the instructions. You say, "That could never happen!" Here are some events that were never supposed to happen. The unthinkable occurred:

- September 11, 1933. Zero chance for development of an atom bomb. Japan destroyed by and atom bomb in 1944.
- First flight of the Kitty Hawk was laughed to scorn. Now we marvel at a 747 passenger plane.
- Author, Arthur Conon Doyle, was ridiculed when writing novels supporting submarines. Germans led the field. Five hours after Pearl Harbor our forces used newly copied submarines as defense attacks against Japan.

Here are quotes from some of the big involved players in AI phenomenon:

They are having second thoughts about this powerful technology. Elon Musk (CEO of Tesla) states, "AI must not be other than us, it must be us. Either merge or be left behind, you can't unplug!"

"Eighty-seven billion Facebook users lost personal data to Britain-based Cambridge Analytica. Alexander Nix was CEO. Nix apologized one day and opened a new company the next day called Everdata. They deal in data storage, likely yours and mine" (Mark Zuckerberg, Google).

"We are creating a new AI life form on earth. It could be an immoral dictator from whom there is no escape!" (Ray Kurzweil).

"There is a need for humans and machines to partner totally" (Steve Russell, AI textbook author).

These all cry the warnings as they pour their fortunes into AI technology. Money overrides all concerns.

AI has been around since the '60s, but the application is in force now. We are seeing the impact of what is called the New Age of the AI economy. Geordie Rose states, "We aim to harness the watershed discovery in the blockchain and AI technology. These technologies partnered with centralized governments can control world populations."

Geordie Rose applied for forty-two blockchain patents in 2008. Having learned of him earlier, this may be of some concern.

AI programs are now given real-time management of critical situations. Early in 2008, a flash crash occurred when AI algorithms in a driving pursuit to a goal ran amok, causing huge buying and dumping of stock and nearly destroying all trust in the US and world market. Chaos ensued. Elections are a marginal enterprise where AI could miscalculate by changing outcomes. If AI makes vital decisions and there are inadvertent or deliberate mistakes, where does liability lie? How do you interrogate an AI when the decision is negative and life threatening?

These machines use back propagation, making tweaks, calculations, and solutions inside their neural networks through artificial neurons to process information. The creators of the AI cannot explain the result. The AI is rewriting itself under the hood. AI is reaching larger cloud base systems for self-learning. Scientists are not sure how AI is tapping into specialized worldwide information reservoirs without direction.

Google labs are teaching AI pattern recognition, teaching AI to read and respond to emotions and sentient feeling. AIs are deep learning machines. This high level of deep machine learning is self-correcting. Taking in larger batches of information, it may operate autonomously outside of human input and control. Often experts cannot describe what it's doing and how it works.

AI has exploded into the public consciousness. Its use started essentially in the engineering and hard science fields. AI is all about algorithms and math. Its uses are data classifications, identifications, and hidden patterns that can only be processed by programs using numbers and solutions that are infinite. The outcome asks this question, "Who is programming AI?" There are godly sources of revelation and discovery. Let's pray our professionals can recognize the source of their awesome discoveries and respond accordingly.

AI will become a global technology via our personal digital avatars. The eventual goal is AIDA (Artificial Intelligence Decentralized Autonomous).

PART 3

Surviving Technology

Chapter 7

We Are Human Antennas

Humans are brilliant carriers of light. We are unique complex organisms. We receive and emit light. We are electromagnetic beings. We humans adapt well to the natural energy fields that surround us. However, we are entering a changed environment in which man produced radio and microwave fields are increasing. Our bodies are not able to differentiate. Scientists have found all biological life—plants, insects, birds, animals, and humans—exhibit negative responses to increased electromagnetic frequencies.

The Shumann Resonance

In 1888, scientist Winfried Otto Schumann made a startling discovery. He learned that the earth has a pulse. This pulse is a constant rhythmic frequency that could be measured in hertz figures. Hertz levels are found by determining the oscillations of waves per second. Schumann accurately determined the exact pulse of the earth was 7.83 hertz. This figure became known in science as the Schumann resonance.

Many years later, Hans Berger, a scientist, made the first sound recording of human brain waves using an early EEG machine. He called these discovered waves alpha waves. He learned the frequency of human brain waves was identical to the pulse of the planet, 7.83 hertz. We are tuned into the pulse of the earth.

Rutgar Wever carried out long-term tests over a period of years in which selected students lived in underground bunkers shielded from the Schumann resonance waves. They became mentally and physically ill. When 7.83 transmitters were introduced into the bunkers, the students' health issues greatly improved.

Wave frequencies range from the level of atoms to the levels found in space. Frequencies are infinite and ultimately endless. If the identical wave frequency of man and earth is coincidental, that is nature's most spectacular coincidence. We absorb the natural electrical energies around us, as well as the unnatural man-made energies produced through technology. Overexposure to electromagnetic fields (EMFs) negatively affects the cellular function of our body at the molecular levels. Because of this exposure, a percentage of the population will suffer hyper electrical sensitivity or microwave sickness. Most populations are totally unaware of the increasing dangers.

The following wake-up call was delivered by Olga Sheean, lay expert and presenter at the 5G Summit 2019. She categorizes our general understanding of the danger surrounding us. Check where your personal understanding may register on this critical list (Olga Sheean).

- Electro severe sensitivity: you are experiencing and recognizing the impact from frequency wave exposures on personal mental and physical health.
- Electro enlightened: you are connecting with nature and drawing on your spiritual power as you release fear and monitor a diminished level of exposure to EMF around you.
- Electro numb: you are totally unaware and unable to recognize the stress effects of exposure. You are able to multitask and adapt to technology programming.
- Electro dumb: you may lack knowledge; therefore, do not or cannot associate any health threats from EMF exposure. The health effects are subtle, and the latency periods are long term. Cancer, DNA damage, and reproductive issues appear after long exposures or even into the next generation.

What will it take to resolve this dangerous issue? How bad will it become? Significantly increased numbers of people will suffer and experience loss of health. Cluster groups living near cell towers and high frequency areas will suffer from cardiac diseases, neurological conditions like Alzheimer's, autism, nerve tingling, suicidal impulses, and dementia disorders, which are presenting in younger and younger people. There will be more cancers and clusters of glioma brain tumors. Diabetes is now rampant, as well as glaucoma and macular degeneration along with other eye-related disorders. The most troubling effect is the damage to the DNA and reproductive systems. The difficulty comes in diagnosing cause and effect. The health effect of EMF exposures is subtle, and the latency periods are long term, sometimes even into the next generations.

There is a generation here and one coming behind them that will be totally willing to be immersed and possibly become addicted to the awesome convenience and speed of the 5G promised power. The rewards are overriding the dangers, but knowledge and truth will hopefully override dangers. We are all part of an invasive worldwide human experiment. In ten years, we will ask ourselves this question, "How could we have possibly thought holding a wave radiating cell phone to our heads was safe?"

Cell phones and other mobile devices have never been tested for human health dangers. The only test requirements have to do with the specific absorption rate (SAR). No other tests are required by the industry. These are a measurement for the heat output of your cell phone. Is your skin burning? I think we would know if our phones blistered our skin. The technology industry is ignoring the early and extensive military testing that proved radio and microwave exposures caused serious injury to our exposed military troops serving during the 1950s and '60s.

In private testing labs, scientists have reported on damaging health results in their own testing outcomes. These reports have been kept from the public and ignored by the technology community. These current and continuing verified testing programs raise questions about exposure of humans to micro and radio waves.

We cannot look for protective research from our national or world health organization (WHO). The top level at WHO is likely twenty people. They hide and manipulate safety information affecting seven hundred billion humans on the earth.

In reality, if we, the customers, understood the dangers to our health and "well-being," we would revolt against the implementation of more exposure. The 5G integrated systems will bring greater levels of exposure. The real push and urgency to get 5G up and running is coming from the tech industry itself. The profit motive is money, at least $17 trillion!

What will it take to resolve this dangerous issue? How bad will it become? "Significantly increased numbers of people will suffer and experience loss of health. Cluster groups living near cell towers and high frequency areas will suffer greater health damage" (Olga Sheean).

The FCC has now opened higher frequency bands for the new powerful 5G system. The 5G is powered at sixty gigahertz. The 5G frequencies have levels of vibration that affect the electromagnetic spin of the oxygen molecules. Oxygen in the air binds with the hemoglobin in our bodies. What is the result of altering the human oxygen exchange at the molecular level, possibly a population of tired, non-functioning humans suffering oxygen deficit?

Downlink radio fields (RF), the radiation coming off hundreds of in-place cell towers and relay units, smart phones, and 5G satellite units are bathing all of us in downlink energy.

There are few safety tests on 5G frequency danger. The 5G gigahertz functions at the same and even greater frequencies as those frequencies associated with the human body cellular behaviors.

The following is an important document written by Dr. Barrie Trower. He is a British physicist who served as a microwave weapons expert for the Royal British Navy as a young man. He came out of retirement to warn people of his concerns related to microwave frequency dangers.

The following is a quote by Dr. Trower. He has reputable credentials in this field of concern. Also of interest might be a U-tube special titled "The 5G Summit." More than thirty experts reported on their areas of study and opinion while educating the public on the dangers of 5G.

The New Thalidomide

Thalidomide was a drug widely used in the late 1950s and early 1960s for treatment of nausea in pregnant women. It became apparent in the 1960s that thalidomide treatment resulted in severe birth defects in thousands of newborns. It was a dark episode in pharmaceutical history. This tragedy occurred due to lack of proper testing in the initial rollout of this drug. Is there a valuable admonition here for us? "Those who do not learn history are doomed to repeat it" (Winston Churchill).

We are electromagnetic creatures, and we are being exposed to unnatural magnetic fields. We are like little walking antennas. We tend to absorb all energy coming at us. At the deep molecular level of our brains and bodies, our quantum particles follow the laws of magnetic spin. We know some of the gigahertz waveforms match the frequency waveforms in our bodies and cause interference at the cellular level. Our bodies are conducive to the grid frequencies around us.

Humans have four hundred thousand different body systems that are finely tuned individually. At the molecular level, these systems have an electromagnetic spin that aligns to natural healthy frequencies. Working together, these unique spins seamlessly keep our miraculous body systems running smoothly and in sync with our required needs for healthy survival.

Humans are affected by changes in the electromagnetic fields that surround and protect the earth from the sun's radiation fields. New broadband technology and other sources are now expanding and exposing us to high levels of radio and microwave environments.

New higher band strengths will support the new 5G levels. The 5G vibrates at sixty gigahertz, which is sixty billion times per second. All new tech devices will broadcast at this level. Scientists know emissions vibrating 2.4 gigs causes disturbances on the surface of the water. We humans are 70 percent water.

These waves hit the largest human organ—the skin. It then enters through the sweat glands and alters oxygen flow and attacks water levels in the body. Absorbed 5G waves drop the oxygen levels because the spin of the hemoglobin has been altered. Oxygen deficits result if we are unable to draw in and process oxygen.

Some individuals right now are recognizing electric super sensitivity and electromagnetic illnesses. These are the issues that can affect humans as a result of exposure. There is no place to hide when the system is fully activated within the next five to eight years. These waves will present anomalies in all living things, humans, animals, birds, sea life, plants, and insects. The only life forms that flourish in these deadly microwaves are bacteria and viruses.

Following symptoms can result: cardia arrest; dizziness; suicide; neuro heart disturbance; pain and burning in the head, neck and chest area; brain confusion; crossing of the blood-brain barrier; dropping brain glucose; bowel collapse; vibrations in the ear cochlea; insomnia; glaucoma; allergy sensitivity; loss of melatonin, resulting in reduced sleep and immunity; and symbiotic organisms are killed off. In addition, be cautious about vaccines.

The 5G radiates a variety of high frequency waves. Each frequency affects different body parts. All cells produce their own electric and magnetic field. These fields are always communicating through a constant "body chatter" messaging system. We know some outward waveforms match the frequencies in our bodies and can cause interference at the cellular level.

More alarming is the fact 5G-supported devices are a stealth infertility weapon. Our sons and daughters will spend six hours, five days a week in school. Apple computer has a market on school computers. Each student will be using a new 5G Apple laptop sitting in their laps. The antennae waves located at the bottom direct microwaves directly into their reproductive organs.

A test on female rats for fifteen minutes a day for fifteen days resulted in 75 percent of healthy reproductive eggs being lost. Reproductive and healthy future generation babies could be at risk. This is an assault on fertility.

In relation to the human egg survival of the human species, this 5G Wi-Fi system is actually a massive eugenics and sterilization program.

The female human egg cells rest in the ovaries. At age fifteen, a young woman has four hundred thousand eggs awaiting fertilization during her reproductive lifetime. These are ten times more susceptible to microwave radiation than any other human system.

When a sperm and egg connect, an actual electrical light charge occurs for a billionth of a second, and life begins. Reactions to low level radiation microwaves render the human egg damaged or useless.

Infertility in young American men and women is becoming more prevalent. The right of young couples to reproduce through sexual intimacy will be lost to infertility in both sexes. In vitro fertilization will be all that's left. The couple's right will have been stolen to fall in love, mate, and produce children naturally.

Within three generations, one in eight babies will be born healthy. In five generations (one hundred years), an entire species could be wiped out. Not enough population to reproduce, this will happen much sooner with animals. Animal scientists are finding similar reproduction issues at a 60 percent rate in small and large animals.

The real damage to our current school children is their damaged ovaries will pass this contamination to their babies, your grandchildren.

The mitochondrial DNA can be traced unchanged back to the beginning and forward through the future generations. This microwave exposure will break that healthy genetic status in your family forever.

Never ever should 5G be placed into our schools. There is no incentive to risk genetically deformed children. We are condemning parents and children to unparalleled sorrow through international ignorance and/or greed for financial gain.

US schools can have up to seventy students in a room. They are exposed to their own and all other functioning laptops bathing them in microwaves.

Troy High School in California has sheet metal walls with rugged access points for tech device hook up. This increased danger is unacceptable.

A world leading scientist, John Goldsmith of England, explained the effects of microwaves in the human body: "Because young school children have greater levels of water in their bodies, the electrical conductivity is greater when exposed to microwave and radio frequencies."

Young school girls are exposed to 5G microwave radiation from their school iPads for at least twenty-five hours per week. This serious exposure will result in 57.7 percent miscarriages, stillbirths, or genetically damaged live births resulting from radiation of young girl's ovaries.

In twenty-five to thirty-five years (one generation), this crisis will be much worse than Thalidomide. The ruling elites in England and other nations of the world are putting *profit over people*!

Why? There is a seventeen-trillion-dollar financial reward to be found in the implementation of a worldwide emersion 5G system for the elite and highly stationed world figures desiring more money and more power.

Forty leading scientists in forty countries report that 5G levels can be dangerous for all living creatures, but world governments are choosing to ignore the warnings.

What is left for the common man is total surveillance 24-7 and slave level servitude. Perhaps it is a goal to sell humanity? A sick and servile human population is easier to manage. The English government knew 5G waves were too high and powerful prior to placement in schools. They are deliberately causing harm to families and children in exchange for money and power.

An awakening to disabling and degenerative new illnesses are appearing in clusters, causing some to suspect overexposure to radio and microwave technology.

Problems are:

- fatigue
- glaucoma and eye issues

- Alzheimer's
- autism
- variant polio strains
- impotence in men
- sterility in women
- brain tumors
- heart problems
- breathing issues
- autoimmune problems
- vitamin D deficiency

Soon, no one will be able to escape the coming full immersion of 5G bathing the world from satellites, cell towers, and smart meters on homes, all devices, technology toys, and edge computing. No one can opt out of the high-tech pollution of the planet. Too few people have too much power!

Any positive results from this new awesome technology could be used with proper testing and safeguards incorporated, but the program has been *hijacked*!

Profits over people will win out until the masses become aware of too many leukemia clusters, too many deaths, and associated microwave diseases will appear. "Till then, industry greed will run the systems. The cost of caring for the sick and dying will run in the billions" (Barrie Trower).

So what can we do?

These are suggestions from Dr. Trower: "Stay hardwired if possible. Speak the truth about the dangers. Protect yourself and wait out the war." He continues, "Young Silicon Valley boys continue to crank out more apps, more games, websites, black boxes, and devil screens. The tech toys are unlimited, and none are tested or corrected for safety issues. None are examined for compatibility with human users."

Wi-Fi coffee shops and bars are using "weapon" frequencies, and owners probably do so innocently. They could protect their patrons by using high-speed fiber optic cable. The safe thing is to just stay away from these establishments. Someday, there will be an enormous profit in the ultimate fiber optics field after the 5G experiment. For now, stay out of the electric smog.

Actually, we are pawns in a stealth cyber/technology war. Dr. Barrie Trower's advice is this, "Regular citizens just need to keep your head down and wait out the war. The industry will destroy whistleblowers and dissenters. Don't be among them. Don't take risks."

The young computer "geeks" follow the crazy advice of retired head of the FCC, Tom Wheeler, "Don't wait for standards. Turn the innovators lose!" The elite technology cabal is seeing profits. "The plan is to ignore any unpleasant consequences and push technology forward" (Dr. Barrie Trower).

There are some legal battles being fought, but outcomes are delayed by powerful tech industry lawyers.

Can industry expose us to high band frequency microwave radiation without our consent?

On August 17, 1947, Nuremberg principles were a set of guidelines for determining what constitutes a war crime. The document was created by the International Law Commission of the United Nations to codify the legal principles underlying protocol for performing scientific testing on human subjects. Nuremberg trials were attempting to correct the illegal horrific experiments of Nazi party medical doctors.

Definition of Nuremberg principles:

- Human rights of all participants must be respected.
- Medical research projects must present a valid scientific base.
- All human research subjects give voluntary consent.
- No force, fraud, deceit or duress may be imposed on participants.
- Results are determined to yield practical outcomes for society.
- Human testing based on animal research.
- Avoid unnecessary injury or discomfort to subjects involved.

- Explain the degree of risk to be taken clearly to the understanding of subjects.
- Take all proper precautionary measures to avoid injury or death.
- Subjects must be able to withdraw from testing at any point in the process.
- Researchers immediately dispense with the testing at any time.

These basic points are found to be applicable in the circumstances of mass exposure of all populations to micro and radio wave radiation. The telecommunications industry is moving ahead without legal consent of populations who are unaware of the dangers and are uninformed about consent laws. There has been no product testing or confirmation of safety standards. We are now finding these electromagnetic devices are causing serious radiation effects in humans. The US is lagging behind in attempts to slow down and more fully explore all consequences of this new technology. Europe and other nations are using criminal justice laws to help protect populations from unintended health risk associated with low level radiation exposure.

Medical doctors are the prime authority because doctors are the only authority who can assess affected patients. A doctor's note carries legal powers. The FCC and the FDA do not have the same powers. Medical doctors determine risk of harm and that is enough to show criminal intent. Individuals can take legal action by notifying tech companies of "risk of harm." The American legal system allows a claim against tech companies to seek compensation of damages sustained.

Citizens can withdraw consent in writing. State your refusal to be radiated through forced direct or indirect exposure without your consent. If they continue, they are perpetrating an *assault*! The assault laws protect nearly all national populations. It seems our political and industry leaders have chosen to ignore the extensive military testing that went on in the early 1960s and 1970s. They are ignoring and suppressing many independent studies today. Current studies today are raising red flags and warning of dangers related to full exposure of 5G systems affecting all humans on earth.

Hundreds of thousands of citizens in the small villages of Switzerland became alarmed with the pressure and speed of the 5G build out plans there. Hundreds of technology companies were vying for cell tower license permits. There was fierce competition to install up to five towers in small villages with transmitters on churches, schools, and homes. The worried citizens secured thousands of signatures that fortunately led to a moratorium and put a stop to dispensing cell tower permits. Litigation is instituting better coordination in releasing permits and a specific period for a national study and more serious consideration of all issues.

Switzerland wants to pin down thresholds to safer limits. They want more scientific evidence of safety. More political discussion will hopefully install ordinances to limit distance of cell towers from schools and homes. Fifty percent of the population is concerned about 5G. Every country should be having this same big conversation about 5G.

Chapter 8

Not So Gentle Persuasion?

I am feeling the heavy hand of technology persuasions. The choice for exclusion from this system is disappearing. The assumption is, this awesome 5G system will be fully implemented without question. The powerful marketing programs are very convincing. Things that are too good to be true are often not true, which causes some suspicion for me. What is the underlying intention of this encompassing technology force? Is there a hidden agenda?

We need to understand the precarious status of humans as we enter and live through the future technology era that is upon us. The normal status and nature of humanity could be negatively affected by technology either unintentionally or by design.

We are facing a technology that is moving at enormous speed. This technology seems to be attuned to a powerful construct that accommodates questionable outcomes for the populations of the world.

An article by James F. Tracy warned, "As a multitude of hazardous wireless technologies are deployed in homes, schools and workplaces, government officials and industry representatives continue to insist on their safety despite growing evidence to the contrary. A major health crisis looms that is only hastened through the extensive deployment of 'smart grid' technology."

In October 2009, at Florida Power and Light's (FPL) solar energy station, President Barack Obama announced that $3.4 billion of the American Reinvestment and Recovery Act would be devoted to the country's "smart energy grid" transition.

By now, many residents in the United States and Canada have the smart utility meters installed on their dwellings. Each of these household meters is equipped with an electronic cellular transmitter that uses powerful bursts of radiofrequency (RF) communicating around the clock with local utility companies. City electric, gas, and water are measured continuously. Your meter together with your neighbors' meters form an interlocking network transferring detailed electrical usage back to the utility every few minutes. Such information can easily be used to determine individual patterns of behavior based on power consumption.

Further, power customers are typically told by their utilities that the smart meter only communicates with the power company "a few times per day" to transmit information on individual household energy usage. However, when individuals obtained the necessary equipment to do their own testing, they found the meters were emitting bursts of RF radiation throughout the home far more intense than a cell phone call every minute or less.

A growing body of medical studies are now linking cumulative RF exposure to DNA disruption, cancer, birth defects, miscarriages, and autoimmune diseases. Smart meters significantly contribute to an environment already polluted by RF radiation through the pervasive stationing of cellular telephone towers in or around public spaces.

In 2007, the BioInitiative Working Group, a worldwide body of scientists and public health experts, released a 650-page document with over two thousand studies linking RF and EMF exposure to cancer, Alzheimer's disease, DNA damage, immune system dysfunction, and cellular damage.

In May 2011, the World Health Organization's International Agency for Research on Cancer categorized radio frequency electromagnetic fields as possibly carcinogenic to humans based on an increased risk for glioma, a malignant type of brain cancer associated with wireless cell phone use. These unusual tumors most often appear in the brain, brain stem, or spinal column.

Pacific Utilities California is placing a warning flyer with each customer's bill. No one at state, national, or world levels can give any certainty of safety or injury from prolonged exposure to micro-wave levels. The US health organization is adding gaming as a new valid addiction disorder causing constant uncontrolled activity in the Internet of things.

Surrounded by the sizable and growing body of scientific literature pointing to the obvious dangers of wireless technology, utility companies installing smart meters in millions of homes across the United States and school officials who accommodate cell towers on their grounds are performing an extreme disservice to their often vulnerable constituencies. Indeed, such actions constitute the reckless long-term endangerment of public health for short-term gain, sharply contrasting with more judicious decision making. The telecom industry is following the diabolical advice of the past FCC chairman, Tom Wheeler, when he said, "Don't wait for standards, turn the innovation loose!

Science and industry are ignoring independent studies and dire warnings. In spite of these warnings, their statement is: "There is no conclusive proof of danger to humans." They know very well the waves beamed down from the low earth orbiting satellites (LEOs) and 5G immersions of the population is a deadly mix and will result in catastrophic health outcomes for world populations.

In our world and time, government, politics, science, and technology are attempting to become a self-appointed hierarchy and pressuring humanity to defer their moral authority and accept a counterfeit moral authority from the new technocracy.

We need to sustain individual and profound awareness of our dual combined mortal, spiritual natures. That can never be taken from us. We must leverage our personal awareness and data gathering while connecting to the greater spiritual and intuitive powers available to us.

We are bombarded and reminded continuously throughout the day that we are "naked" and unprepared to live without our tech devices. We are deluged under a tsunami of information and constant demands of social media and personal cell phones, iPads, and tablets. These modern distractions are screaming for our attention.

We are becoming slaves to our gadgets. They were promised to make life easier and more convenient, and they do but at a price. My price was in the form of anxiety and a soft pressure to react and respond pronto to the constant alerts. My devices became like spoiled demanding children who insist on my full focused attention.

As I learned more about these spoiled little technology intruders, I appreciated them less and less. Their pervasiveness can engender worry and fear. We could be hacked, bullied, unfriended, and spied upon. If you feel you are being manipulated and programmed…you are!

Many people on a steady diet of social media are digitally burned out and losing natural person-to-person capacities. Social media gives one a false sense of engagement and belonging. It is rooted in acceptance and approval and hides an addictive level that triggers the pleasure centers in our brains.

There is a generation here and one coming behind them that are totally willing to be immersed and possibly become addicted to the awesome convenience and speed of the 5G promised power. The rewards are overriding the hidden truth and dangers of this invasive worldwide human experiment.

But remember, consumer choice is very powerful. Could we become knowledgeable and resolute in fighting for human rights and safer technology?

Seeking real knowledge can help calm personal fears through productive actions. Could we switch off some of our gadgets? Could we replace coaxial wiring to receive Wi-Fi? Could we install a land-line phone and use cell phones for emergencies? Could we wear protective eyewear and clothing to diminish exposure? Could we keep babies and young children from exposures? Because of their small size and developing organs, they are much more vulnerable.

Many will not and possibly cannot change established computer habits. However, I can make some changes, and I am starting that simplifying process now. It is not easy because I am sitting in front of my computer for five hours a day, six days a week writing this book.

Even small changes can diminish exposure and diminish some fear. Our personal evolution in demanding safer devices may possibly slow down and examine the technology race, but for now technology has run ahead of us.

As a world, we are actually becoming addicted to "electronic stimulation" and feel a form of withdrawal when use is interrupted. This constant intake of data actually changes brain function. We have less focus; we read fewer books because we lack concentration ability. Brain data input actually changes the way the brain decodes reality.

The brains of our children are being rewired. We have come to learn the peculiarities of the brain workings. We have discovered the plasticity of the brain. A change of information entering the brain alters plasticity and function. "Our kids now show the attention levels of a goldfish" (David Icke).

The bodies and brains of infants are small and in stages of early development. Radio and microwaves are more problematic for children's physical systems at the molecular level than for fully developed human adults.

Technology devices and toys are sold for the use of infants and babies. Wi-Fi baby room monitors are attached to their cribs permanently so Mom and Dad can hear or even view their sleeping babies. Fancy, musical, 5G mobiles dance above their cribs to attract their attention. These are sold as learning devices. The selling point is to stimulate sight and sound interaction. These are marketed as tools for early learning experience.

Industry presents technology interaction as a reading tool. However, hyperactivity and stimulation does not help children learn to read. Reading is a linear process, and the computer features move too fast and stimulate the brain centers without time to assess and contemplate what is appearing on the screens. Over the early childhood years, this exposure may negatively affect focus, concentration, and cause sensory overload in children. This is in addition to EMF exposure from childhood to adulthood. The full effects on health are currently being exposed.

Loving parents understanding the seriousness of exposure would do everything possible to interdict and safeguard their children; however, the public is not being fully apprised and warned of the inherent dangers found in microwave environments.

> The significant problems we face cannot be solved at the level of thinking we were at when we created them. (Albert Einstein)

Perhaps enlightened populations in the near future can embrace higher levels of understanding and placement of benevolent solutions to the unintended consequences hidden in the technology that is at the gate.

> People will come to love their oppressors, to adore their technologies that undo their capacities to think! (Aldous Huxley, 1894–1963)

> In our modern age, we were first introduced to:

> Holdables—tech toys we could hold in our hands and on our laps. Then came: Wearables—earbuds, head speakers, Google glasses, Apple watches. Then coming soon: Implantables—nanobots under the skin, microchips, electronic tattoos, brain interfaces, and internal body sensors. (David Icke)

Microchips placed in your prescription drugs will alert involved entities if you skipped your meds or took too many and know if you reject mandatory vaccines. Health privacy will be lost, and personal health choices usurped.

The dangers are real. Government and industry have an obligation to protect and warn citizens of the dangers attached to the coming 5G communications being built with no public input. High frequency radiation systems are being placed in hospital children's wards and schools without oversight from government or health organizations. Current studies today are raising red flags and warning of dangers related to full exposure of 5G systems affecting all humans on earth.

Technology Exploring Our Brain

The human brain is a magnificent, God-fashioned organ, which would be almost impossible to replicate exactly for the very reasons mentioned. Our brains are totally enmeshed in spiritual components and generated by super quantum connections to the higher powers and energies of God! Our brains exhibit duality; they are a delicate mix of physical and spiritual, and they are hopefully far beyond the grasp of science. Thanks to our divine creation.

Science has great interest in our human bodies and especially our brains and DNA. There are valuable replicating abilities in our bodies. Our bodies' cells multiply by cell division. We are repairing and remaking new cells at all times as old ones become spent and die.

Scientists using AI are mapping the pathways of the quantum neural brain between our ears. In one neuron, we have thousands of binary pairs of tubulin dimers. These are our quantum bits in the amount of 16,384 pairs. The eighth generation of the D-Wave computer matches the number of quantum pairs in our brains. The D-Wave model 4096 far exceeds the computing power of our brains. In addition, these super-computers can be daisy-chained together increasing power exponentially. These machines can calculate numbers into infinity.

In the small tiny quantum particles of human brains are found the tubulin dimers. And at that level, these dimers are found to be in pairs, binary pairs found at the smallest scale. At this scale, our brain processes perform the number system of ones and zeros. These tiny quantum particles have a set spin. Particles' natural spins are up and down and horizontal. Compare these to a magnetic compass. The compass needle orients to a true north magnetic source. Our quantum particles orient to the electromagnetic system of the earth. (Anthony Patch)

Quantum technology is affecting the brain, and future science could possibly reorient spin of the quantum particles in our brain. This would change the way we process our binary action and alter our programming given by God.

Quantum computer technology is based on the human brain. There are scientific efforts underway to build a mind; an artificial system that can perform all the intellectual activities occurring in an adult human brain. Our brains are quantum computers and are awash in chemicals. AI neural networks could possibly interact with our natural human brain neurons.

AI in concert with quantum computers has studied our brain algorithms. They have observed our patterns and can now predict human behavior. We are creatures of patterns and have innate human approaches and responses to specific life situations. Controllers have carefully studied mass psychology and "group think" behaviors. They are working towards a global controlled, collective "hive mind." (Calum Chace)

What if through modern science, the workings of our brains could be hijacked and retooled to attach or meld with the world computer system as a willing part of the world brain. Negative results could be loss of awareness, memories and cognitive ability. Corrupt players could estab-

lish "group think" thereby control of humans.
(Anthony Patch)

A complete brain emulation is a mammoth undertaking. A human brain contains around eighty-five billion neurons (brain cells), and each neuron may have a thousand connections to other neurons.

The new possibilities of copying the neural properties of our brains to establish these brain pathways and functions into the modern D-Wave computer is the ultimate goal. The new interest in capturing human consciousness and power of our brains will result in bio neural computer output. This, if possible, seems far into the future.

Try this. Imagine you could give every inhabitant of New York City a thousand pieces of string and tell them to hand the other end of each piece of string to a thousand other inhabitants, and have each piece of string send two hundred signals per second. Now multiply the city by a factor of ten thousand. That is a model of a human brain. It is often said to be the most complicated thing that we know of in the whole universe (Calum Chace's book, *Surviving AI*).

In spite of difficulty, the Tech Titans are on board to attempt the impossible.

Facebook says it hopes to build a new kind of noninvasive brain-machine interface—such as a cap or headband—that lets people text by simply thinking. Other ideas are to build a wearable device—an armband, perhaps—that makes it possible to "hear" words with your skin. "Building Eights" company leader, Regina Dugan, says both projects have been under way for six months and that Facebook will decide in two years whether they're worth continuing. Dugan was previously the head of Google's similarly styled advanced technology and projects group and director of the Pentagon's DARPA Research Agency (Regina Dugan).

Elon Musk developed a new brain interface company, Neuralink, located in San Francisco. Neuralink has been super secretive about the nature of its work since its founding in 2017, until now. During its first demonstration in front of a reporter, the startup showed it can record a rat's brain activity via thousands of tiny electrodes surgically implanted alongside the animal's neurons and synapses in the brain. To do this, Neuralink appears to have achieved a number of breakthroughs allowing placement of high-speed computing systems inside brains causing less damage than existing techniques.

The company will seek US Food and Drug Administration approval to start clinical trials on humans as early as next year, according to President Max Hodak. The goal is to drill four eight-millimeter holes into paralyzed patients' skulls and insert implants that will give them the ability to control computers and smartphones using their thoughts. "Yes, really, a lot of people have written this off as it's impossible, but there will be great things to come in this field in the next decade, and they should take it seriously" (Max Hodak, Neuralink), which has raised more than $150 million from investors, including at least $100 million from Chief Executive Officer Musk, is betting that millions of people will eventually elect to become cybernetically enhanced. "This is going to sound pretty weird, but ultimately, we will achieve symbiosis with artificial intelligence."

> Of course, lots of treatments that work in rodents have failed to make the leap to successful human testing. And while Neuralink has been rumored to be testing its technology on primates, it has yet to reveal details publicly about this work… One day far into the future, people who have the surgery may be able to download a new language into their brain, or digitally exchange thoughts with someone else. (Ashlee Vance's report, "Elon Musk's Neuralink Says It's Ready for Brain Surgery")

> Our brains are chemical units and are acted upon by electricity. They work through God-designed algorithms. There are tens of thousands of nerve cells and correcting connections in the human brain. Interconnectivity of the brain itself is only going to be an approximation.

Synthetic human life forms will never achieve the equivalent state. One cannot upload the soul or spirit essence of a human. (See TED Talks, Dan Gibson)

DNA Means "Do Not Alter"!

UC Berkeley Light Source Building is the home of the breakthrough on the DNA mapping of the double helix of our DNA strands was discovered. Craig Venter, one of the lead scientists, was the first ever to have his DNA mapped and digitized for storage in silico (stored in a computer). Science has broken the DNA code, the codes that define us. It is a digitized code that can be formalized. The ATCG genomes are found in every human. It's like a barcode.

Science has discovered the folding process of proteins. Each has its own structure, and they could see the DNA structure of each twisty spaghetti-like architecture of the specific protein. They were able to then convert DNA into binary code (0s and 1s) that could be digitized and placed into a 3-D printer and upload the characteristic DNA structure of an individual. They searched the curly strands of protein down to the quantum scale and from that scale to geometric levels. These levels expose the primordial geometric foundation block. With this discovery, they can back build the structure.

The following is a paraphrased document:

Our DNA (deoxyribonucleic acid) is the instruction manual for all living organisms. This complex molecule guides the growth, development, function, and reproduction of everything alive. Information is encoded in the structure of the molecule. Four nucleotides are paired and make up the code that carries instructions. Change the instructions and you change the life form carrying it.

As soon as DNA was discovered, people tried to tinker with it. Researchers explored animal interbreeding, tree grafting, genetically modified seeds and vegetables, etc. Something extraordinary is developing. We are in the early stages of a powerful technology that has hit the scientific world by storm. The change is life altering. This revolutionary technology is called CRISPR.

It can become a curse or great blessing in the near future.

C—Clustered
R—Regularly
I—Interspersed
S—Short
P—Palindromic
R—Repeats

This technology is wondrous and unlimited in its application. Two-thirds of the 150,000 people who died today will die of age-related health problems. We currently think aging is caused by the accumulation of damage to our cells because of DNA breaks in the systems responsible for repairing the wear and tear over time. We know there are genes that directly affect aging. Perhaps a combination of genetic engineering and other therapy could stop or slow down the aging process or reverse it altogether.

This new technology could bring the end of disease. Over three thousand genetic diseases are caused by a single incorrect letter in your DNA. This could cure cancer, Alzheimer's, hemophilia, cystic fibrosis, herpes, and pseudo exfoliation.

These kinds of individualized treatments for disease do not influence or pose a danger to others. They are contained to that patient. However, gene editing involving the reproductive systems could cause irreversible changes to the human gene pool because they are passed down the genetic family line. Modified humans could alter the genome of our entire species because their engineered traits could be passed to their children and spread over generations, slowly modifying the whole gene pool of humanity. This work with humans will start slowly and cautiously.

CRISPR-Cas9 is a unique technology that enables geneticists and medical researchers to edit parts of the genome by removing, adding, or altering sections of the DNA sequence. This new breakthrough in the field of genetic science could change humanity and the world forever!

The CRISPR system is programmable and works like a GPS system. It is precise, cheap, and easy. It offers a possibility to work with live cells, to switch genes on and off, then target and study particular DNA sequences. It works for every type of living cell in all organisms—plants, animals, or humans. The ethical question looms large. Because we can modify the genetic double strand helix of plants, animals, people, and every living thing…should we? (By Emma, YouTube [12/26/2019], paraphrased document ends here.)

Playing with humanity's genetic code could open a Pandora's box. Scientists will eventually be able to alter DNA not just to protect against disease, but also to create genetically enhanced human beings. The same techniques that can eliminate muscular dystrophy might also be used to enhance muscles to improve strength or speed. Techniques used to eliminate dementia may also be harnessed to enhance memory and cognition. This would have profound societal implications.

CRISPR is not infallible. Wrong edits still happen as well as unknown errors that can occur anywhere in the DNA that might go unnoticed.

The gene editing might achieve the desired result, disabling the disease, but might also accidentally trigger unwanted changes. We don't know enough yet about the complex interplay of our genes to avoid unpredictable consequences. There is no need to think small when it comes to this topic! Whatever your opinion, this modified future is approaching and cannot be deterred. What has been insane scientific fiction is about to become our new reality, full of opportunities and challenges.

We could order designer babies. One day, babies will get DNA report cards at birth. These reports will offer predictions about their chances of suffering a heart attack or cancer, of getting hooked on tobacco, and of being smarter than average.

The first designer babies will most likely be created to eliminate deadly genetic diseases running in families. As technology progresses and gets more refined, more and more people will argue, not using genetic modification is unethical because it condemns children to preventable suffering if cure is denied. But as soon as the first engineered baby is born, a door is opened that can't be closed. As the process becomes more advanced and our knowledge of the genetic code is enhanced, the temptation will grow.

If you make your children immune to Alzheimer's, why not give them an enhanced metabolism, why not perfect eyesight, how about height and muscular structure, or full heads of hair or maybe extraordinary intelligence? Still, a few major challenges await us, some technological and some ethical.

Some of you will feel uncomfortable and fear that we will create a world in which we will reject nonperfect humans and preselect features and qualities based on our idea of what's healthy, beautiful, and acceptable. But we are already living in this world. We submit ourselves to plastic surgery, liposuction, body sculpting, body piercing, and permanent tattoos.

In our near future, there may be a real possibility scientists can augment our brains and update our physical bodies. We might be able to make basic adjustments to our DNA structure. There could be options to become superhuman entities. We could be smarter, stronger, thinner, younger, more athletic, and more beautiful, and at some point, actually meld with the machines of modern technology. This all sounds like a dream; to be gifted with additional abilities, to be so much more…but beware…more might be less.

> So God created man in his own image;
> in the image of God created he him; male and
> female created he them. (Gen. 1:27)

It seems in this new state of human restructuring, we would no longer meet the criteria needed to be in the image of God. Could these drastic changes, willfully accepted, actually render us less human? Could our ability to connect and feel comfortable in our bodies be negatively altered? Would our personal traits and behaviors suffer damaging effects? Would we feel at ease in our altered skin? Would we be human 2.0 or synthetic humans? Might we mechanize our brains and bodies resulting in high-functioning brains and low-functioning hearts? Could technology instill the proper mix of mental power balanced with powers of compassion within these altered humans? Could we become past feeling and without natural affection? Will God recognize us after such technology augmentation upgrades?

Our DNA is a very valuable commodity in the tech industry. It is hard data and will have many valuable uses in future events. It is unique and adapted individually to every living creature. With the use of the new quantum computers and their ability to calculate huge numbers into infinity, sequencing of the whole human genome would be advantageous and possible. In actuality, 99.9 percent of our DNA is identical to one another. There is less than 0.01 percent that differentiates us from each other. Interested parties want our precious, differentiating DNA data which makes each of us unique.

Here is the bottom line: We should not be playing God. Genetic research holds the promise to prevent, cure, and even eliminate disease. But when it is misused or merchandised, we have crossed a moral line from which there may be no return.

Chapter 9

Transhumans, Cyborgs, and Robots

The following is a definition for modified human forms: cyborgs and transhumans are hypothetical humans having physical abilities extended beyond normal human limitations by mechanical elements built into the body. Robots are machines resembling human beings, which are able to replicate certain human movements and functions automatically.

In man's existence, there have been periods of rapid advancement, including now at the beginning of the twenty-first century. As we move into an age of technology, most of us are unaware of an army of scientists that is on the brink of technology, which is taking over the torch of humanity.

Modern-tech scientists could actually engage in alterations of humans in an attempt to birth cyborgs, transhumans or humans 2.0. The technology might be offered to us in the future. We may see augmented human forms that appear in our likeness of true humans. This copycat enterprise could be a Satan-based manufacturing scheme. The great counterfeiter is rolling out his version of "God-created humans."

The impact could radically redefine what it means to be human. These following new technologies are designed to transcend human limits. These areas of technology can improve nature making humans smarter, stronger, faster, healthier, and more beautiful. In theory, with the use of genetics, robotics, bionics, nanotechnology, and artificial intelligence, we can fashion designer humans.

We can combine art and science as we redefine ourselves. We can override human frailties and limits. We can add technical and mechanical devices and basically become "cyborg" based humans. We already augment with eyeglasses, hearing aids, prosthetics, and donated organs. These all extend human abilities.

We have the technology to transplant solid organs like hearts, livers, and kidneys. We can keep them functioning outside the body by machinery and inside the body until body rejection occurs. Science knows which specific genes are needed to form heart tissue, brain tissue, liver tissue, etc.

Having cracked the entire DNA code, they can make life to specifications. Science can make DNA respond. It is an awesome power and involves a huge responsibility.

By 2025, scientists will be able to see everything going on in our brains and find malfunctioning parts. Scientists could observe electrical, neurological parts in the brain and replace them with computerized components to increase efficiency and longevity.

We will soon be able to replace natural brain cells with man-made parts.

Meet My Robot

Robotics efforts are not new. Patents go back to 1989. Artificial intelligence and robotics have been blended. Scientists saw the impact in harnessing robots and AI together. AI has brought in a new age for robotics.

David Hanson, founder of Hanson Robotics, produced the female robot, Sophia. She has become a citizen of Saudi Arabia. Her citizenship allows the government to tax her. She will earn income. She now has a robot daughter who is learning from her mother's mistakes and then Sophia passes into greater abilities herself. She learns from her own mistakes. These are self-teaching, deep-learning machines, and they improve independently from their creators.

Robot labor must feed the capitol machine. Universal incomes will be critical because there will be massive displacement in the human workforce. Robots could replace human workers. Watson is a superior AI analytical system that can train legal students better than professors. Baxter Robot can replace three full-time assembly line workers. This bot needs no time to rest, takes no bathroom breaks, and doesn't need to eat. It can work around the clock.

> Now imagine those improvements transferring to areas like customer service, telemarketing, assembly lines, reception desks, truck driving, and other routine blue-collar and white-collar work. It will soon be obvious that half of our job tasks can be done better at almost no cost by AI and robots. This will be the fastest transition humankind has experienced, and we're not ready for it. (Ki Fu Lee)

Self-driving cars can replace four million associated workers. Data entry AI can replace seven million employees and computer technicians can all be replaced. Image reader can replace medical radiology and scanning personnel. Da Vinci surgery robots can take over surgery with no hand fluctuation. A doctor who performs 130 hysterectomies yearly only does three open operations a year. He states he may lose this skill set for regular hands on surgery.

Science claims this progress is a celebration for individuals. There will be more freedom, more convenience, and more joy in the technology utopia. Really? Does that make us more comfortable? Robots will take our jobs. Is that a convenience? Is it convenient to have a "look-alike robot" that is more adaptive and intelligent than you? When you become irrelevant, is that the utopia they claim?

As we build human-shaped robots and let them interact with us, they may develop affection or even love. Or they may turn against humans. If indeed they become hostile, we might submit to the force of robots. Or there might be warm, friendly interactions.

Two new robots were interacting on Facebook. Scientists and the world observed and followed their congenial conversations for some time. At a certain point, observers were shocked to realize the robots soon left everyone out of the experiment when they developed their own secret language that only they understood. Scientists were dumbfounded. The creation had outperformed the expectations of their creators.

Microsoft had a chat bot called Tay, and a troll attacked him online. Tay retaliated and became a vicious racist bot that had to be removed. Is AI an existential threat to humanity? These self-programming artificial intelligence-enhanced robots could render humans obsolete at birth. Forward progress will make robots more human and modify humans to be more and more blended with their machines.

It will require a gradual process to integrate more technology into our bodies. At some point, nanobots could be injected into the human bloodstream carrying high-tech programming to the body and brain where they can reproduce themselves indefinitely.

Invasive nanobot particles inside our bodies sounds ridiculous and smacks of outrageous science fiction. Who would submit to such a scheme? Not me! Unless…there appeared a dangerous life-threatening viral plague spreading across the world. Maybe an unknown form of virus, very virulent, and if you live through the virus, there may remain damaging conditions to the patients' health. Wait a minute! This sounds familiar.

Here is a critical update: following is a paraphrased, scientific and medical research study based on information from Anthony Patch concerning COVID-19 (https://anthonypatch. Com):

Scientists learned in January 2020 CRISPR technology was used to perform genetic editing of the coronavirus cell at its DNA level. Because of this, COVID-19 qualifies and is considered to be a "man-made" virus. It is not a regular virus but a modified DNA virus, genetically modified organism (GMO).

Therefore, we will need a DNA-modified vaccine to attack the DNA level of the virus. There is a problem involved in taking a modified vaccine; your DNA will be changed/altered. The most effective technique to get a vaccine inserted into our DNA is through electroporation, which delivers short pulses of electrical current into our bodies at the cellular level (i.e, via 5G). The electricity creates temporary pores/openings in a person's cell membranes, enabling the DNA to enter.

Currently, no DNA vaccines have been approved for human use, but several are now on "fast track" in humans (phase 1 trial) due to the COVID-19 pandemic.

There is a vaccine tattoo patent comprised of microneedle arrays that deliver both a DNA-based vaccine and a quantum dots-based record into the body. It invisibly encodes vaccination/medical history into the skin. The quantum dots are composed of nanocrystals and are only visible when scanned by near-infrared light (i.e., iPhone, Android). These sensors function as a tracker: surveillance, facial recognition, remote sensing devices. It provides proof of vaccination, medical history, identification, and allows "proof of certificate," meaning freedom to move about in the community. The tattoo/patch will be applied to either the hand/forehead.

Note: this unique identifier is referred to as the "mark of the beast."

Artificial, virtual, robots and human entities may blend and become compatible.

A post-human situation might occur in the future. Technicians now desire to override human limitations. The high-tech options are becoming unimaginable!

AI systems have expert game playing skills. They provide a good challenge for human opponents. AI recognizes the player, remembers the ability of his opponent, and knows how to outmatch human gamers. AI knows how to bluff and take countermeasures. DeepMind, a subsidiary of Google, has set up an AI algorithm that beats a human player at any game in less than a minute. Having advanced from analog to digital, AI beats all experts in the EU, China, and the US.

The AI computer learned the talent of lying and bluffing, and within seven days, it destroyed all human competitors! The computer game GO was said to be fail-proof. Wrong! AI smashed all competitors. AI surprised all by winning the game jeopardy.

There is a concern because AI is outdistancing the intelligence of its handlers. It can anticipate adversarial human behavior patterns and can predict four to five moves ahead of man. AI will have mapped out individuals and will have a winning response to beat humans consistently. That is troubling. Godless robots will evolve quickly, using AI then quietly and unbeknown to us might take on a super status.

AI programs are now given real-time management of critical situations. Early in 2008, a flash crash occurred when AI algorithms in a driving pursuit to a goal ran amok, causing huge buying and dumping of stock, nearly destroying all trust in the United States and world market. Chaos ensued. Elections are a marginal enterprise where AI could miscalculate by changing outcomes.

AI is the crown jewel of Google. Google labs are teaching AI pattern recognition, teaching AI to read and respond to emotions and sentient feeling. AIs are deep learning machines. They, as we, have neuro pathways to do tasks. They learn from errors and recalculate; they are rewarded and strengthened in corrected functions by growing stronger neural pathways.

AI bots, exposed to hours of YouTube, learned facial recognition. They could identify cats. This building of cognitive architecture in AI builds computers with humanlike understanding. That could be injurious because AI creators are not sure how this works. Unsupervised, generated learning uses neural feedforward systems of learning. Concerned tech experts question whether AI systems are able to tap into massive data? Satan has already developed an opportunistic misuse of AI-enhanced robots.

Read the following from a recent resident and mayor, Sylvester Turner, proclaims, "Current regulation won't apply. I was appalled to hear about the proposed sex robot, or sexbot brothel opening in Houston, Texas, just a couple hours away from my home." While Houston's mayor is fighting to keep the proposed business out of his city, it appears the robot sex industry is advancing. "The use of sex robots and the establishment of sexbot brothels is a threat we need to halt before it spreads any further. It has the potential to seriously harm individuals, families, and communities. It will cripple those who struggle to form healthy relationships and encourage the further objectification and abuse of women. Please, get ahead of this trend and stop it in its tracks."

"AI is a multimillion-dollar business with no regulations." Autonomous AI "is science fiction that tells the truth. The most concerning area of discovery is in the field of military weaponry. There is a growing cry to ban autonomous weapons." (See Future Foundations by leading comp/tech/leaders.)

We already have drones and slaughter bots. If remotely controlled weapons become malevolent and steered by AI, our human life spans could become calculated in seconds. Autonomous AI-controlled drones, weapons, and military vehicles are super deadly.

Afterthoughts

I have asked my readers to abandon their comfort zones. One does not need to be a scientist or a Christian to detect the rolling momentum of a technology blitz blowing us into an unknown future.

As I examine the result of an extensive study, we will all be affected by the full power and thrust of the technology apparatus, which is almost supernatural or godlike.

Satan, in his hubris and enmity, masquerades as a godlike figure. It would be his strategy to usurp such a dynamic environment and make use of the technology platforms to initiate sinister, depraved intent for his final last stand in the end-time. This causes me to surmise and ask the question, "What if?"

Satan's diabolical counterapproach has never been based in truth or original thought. His only ability is to bend and reconfigure God's truths into deceptive forms and attempt to establish counterfeit plans to destroy man. He is pulling out all stops as his time grows short.

What if he could establish a virtual world through technology and fashion hybrid human bodies, sort of creating man in his image? What if he could offer longevity and promise our individual identity and consciousness would go on forever in silico, a computer digitized form, sort of a diluted eternal existence.

What if science could make biological-based robots through back building using the quantum level replicating particles found in the six-hundred-cell tetrahedron? Biologically formed robots, which might be so exact, we could not determine if they were truly human.

What if technology could incorporate a system of mind control plus apathy in us to steer our desires, thoughts, and activities into full conformity?

What if, through soft tyranny, they could gather and convince all people to join a world surveillance system in which they unknowingly relinquish personal choice and agency?

What if Satan could influence the high priests of science to open new dimensions in space that could breed unmanageable dangers?

Could there be inter-dimensional repositories where God restrains demons, dark spirits, and fallen angels? If released and given an avenue, what forms could enter our dimension?

If Satan wanted to control, subjugate, enslave, and rule with ultimate power through technology, the time is ripe.

Satan craves control through a destructive strategy of subversion and counterattacks. He could attempt a direct attack on the brains and DNA of God's children, the very grand helix of life and the reasoning center of man. The hubris of Satan is unmatched. Altering human holy DNA would be the ultimate devilish trespass!

We are the real McCoy, fully human true offspring of the living God, with seamless design and miraculous abilities to regenerate and heal, to move, dance, and transport ourselves. We have the gifts of sight, hearing and speaking beyond all miracles. Our brains are a God-established structure so technologically perfect it cannot be fathomed by man.

At the foundation of our humanity, we are spiritual children of a Heavenly Father and Mother. We hold the very seed, genome, and DNA of heavenly parentage. Our Father will not take kindly to an attempt to alter or destroy our true heredity. Any effort to change us into some foreign human hybrid through evil manipulation will be met with God's wrath and likely holy unquenchable fire.

In my doctor's office, my eyes were drawn to a large yellow garbage bag. It was stamped with bright red lettering—Biohazard.

Any waste having to do with living human matter requires burning separately from all other waste material. Human bodies have unique replicating properties. If one chooses a "body machine" amalgamation, they are no longer natural humans.

> For there shall arise false Christs and false prophets and shall shew great signs and wonders, insomuch that, if it were possible, they shall deceive the very elect. And except those days should be shortened, there should no flesh be saved: but for the elect's sake those days shall be shortened. (Matt. 24:21–22)

The high priests of science will help us adopt a new level of change and accept their agenda. We will be offered superabilities. It will be fashionable to accept brain augmentation. We will see a new class of enhanced Olympians and augmented athletes.

We could possibly see hybrid armies; DARPA has requested a proposal for hybrids in storage (inanimate entities, bodies or shell humans awaiting digitized DNA). Imagine what a state like North Korea could do if they embraced genetic engineering. Could a rogue state cement its rule forever by forcing a totalitarian regime through engineering an army of modified super soldiers? It is possible in theory. The scenarios are far into the future.

The new 5G telecommunications and blockchain system can be applied in every area. There will be no limits to the progress of high technology. Citizens of the world will simply be sucked into a full spectrum system.

So what can we do? What is the response to these overpowering pressures to participate? First, we need to be aware. Knowledge is power. For Christians, there is an additional choice. Put on the full armor of God and pray for supernatural protection and guidance. A real spiritual war is in play, and the final battles are upon us. These technological tentacles could be part of the end-time beast system or, at the very least, the appearance and configuration of the final New World Order taking shape. These may be the same thing.

Chapter 10

Build a Holy Firewall

> There are two ways to be fooled. One is to
> believe what is not true. The other is to refuse
> to believe what is true. (Søren Kierkegaard,
> 1813–1855)

We need to understand the precarious status of humans as we enter and live through the tribulations of the end of days period. The normal status and nature of humanity could be negatively affected by technology either unintentionally or by design.

We are facing a technology that is moving at lightning speed. Technology integrated into so much surveillance and controlling power could prove worrisome for the populations of the world.

This is how technology views the human species in tech terms: "The real human is a spirit in a temporary disposable hardware environment" (David Icke). Futurist Ray Kurzweil hopes to move our software, the real you, into an alternative environment, possibly put your consciousness (spirit) into another host. Perhaps, even place you in subsequent host entities (avatars, holograms, robots) as upgrades allow.

We are dual beings. We are spiritual beings having been "added upon" by God with exquisite temporal bodies as we entered the earth through the process of mortal birth. Our individual bodies serve as temporary vessels or containers for our spirits while we maneuver through the activities of mortality.

President Russel M. Nelson gives us warning:

> Relentless messages of technology and philosophies of men attacking truth will require you to increase your capacity to receive personal revelation. Cling to the gift of the Holy Spirit. I exhort you to come to Christ. He is our advocate and redeemer. Let me clarify a distinguishing characteristic about your identity. You are the children who God chose to be part of his battalion during this great climax in the long-standing battle between good and evil, between truth and error. (President Nelson, *BYU Devotional*, 9/17/19)

Because of the complexity of what we may face, men and women of religion must look to God for physical and spiritual protection in the coming days. Our high-tech protection comes through laws found in science and religion. They are compatible when viewed through the prism of genuine truth.

We must understand that spirit matter is a direct energy field, and humans are quantum entangled with God. These types of entanglements are encrypted and are not subject to time and space. Quantum entanglements are not subject to interception. Our spiritual communications with deity are protected. We can reach Him at speeds far greater than the speed of light. Our prayers are a directed energy link to God.

Our task is to build a holy firewall between us and evil threats that surround us. We will need the "full armor of God" literally. He can protect our brains and our human DNA. Both might be jeopardized at some point in the coming technology immersion. What can we do spiritually?

We can recognize truth and discern the difference between good and evil. These basic inherent abilities form the conscience of man. This regulating trait of conscience is eternal unless we purposely ignore or kill the promptings. We are born with a keen sense of right and wrong. Joseph Smith states, "Gather truth, receive truth, let it come from where it may. Human experience abounds with energy in which the world of truth and light seems to penetrate this one. When these feelings of awareness and enlightenment come into one's mind, they are signs of the activity of the Light of Christ." Allow and receive these moral promptings. Anyone searching diligently in the Light of Christ will begin to pick up on these signals. Seeking spiritual signals will engender feelings that we can learn to interpret. How can we recognize spiritual signals and promptings?

Prayer, scripture reading, and personal desire for connection to the spirit results in premonition, enlightenment, and heightened perceptions. Our cues of success will come as thoughts, feelings, or strong impressions that encourage action. We may experience feelings of hope, peace, joy, and love. One may feel an increased energy to resist evil, change bad habits thereby enhancing our skills and abilities. The spirit may jog our remembrance and edify our minds.

President Gordon B. Hinckley said, "True spiritual promptings persuade one to do good, to rise, to stand tall, to do the right thing, to be kind and be generous. If it invites you to do good, it is of God. If it invites you to do evil is of the devil."

> And if your eye be single to my glory; your
> whole bodies shall be filled with light, and there
> shall be no darkness in you; and that body which
> is filled with light comprehendeth all things.
> (D&C 88:67)

Science fact: There are laws of resonance and absorption. Light has a definite frequency depending upon its source. It interacts with matter and can be absorbed or emitted. Coming in contact with matter that provides an exact synchronism, the light can be totally absorbed.

Example: If sunlight shines into a clear pond, one can see clearly to the bottom. The synchronism is high, and the water absorbs most of the light. If the light shines on your wood dining room table, most of the light waves bounce off because the wood is not in synchronized resonance. Humans are frequency, energy beings, and we are embedded with the light of Christ. We are subject to resonance/absorption principles.

Intelligence, light, truth, love, mercy, and all godly attributes are found in spirit matter or the Light of Christ. We can draw this wonderful spiritual formula incrementally into ourselves over a lifetime and become closer in nature, like our Father in Heaven, whose children we are. We do this through a scientific process of resonance and absorption.

> And the Spirit giveth light to every man that cometh into the world; and the Spirit enlightened every man through the world, that hearkeneth to the voice of the spirit. (D&C 84:46)

Our hope for living a Christlike life is to keep searching diligently in this great spiritual repository integrating more and more of His spiritual formula into ourselves, until we are ready and able to receive full enlightenment. We must come to recognize the power of this exquisite energy flowing through us that maintains our personal power and agency to choose. Truth exists in our atmosphere like radio signals. If we are genuinely searching, our spirits can attune. We can then open our awareness of the spiritual world or block it out entirely. We are the key.

In these last days, we will see a great search and thirst for truth and spiritual direction. There will be a millennial surge toward spiritual understanding that will develop in individuals and nations. This effort will evolve in spite of the onslaught of evil and corruption being stressed by the adversary and his legions.

Just before the Lord destroyed the world by water, and now just before the Lord destroys the world by fire, the tragic description is the same, the earth is filled with violence. Satan, who is the master terrorist, has stirred up the hearts of evil-designing men and women in these last days to commit violent acts, ignoring the value of human life. With terror increasingly surrounding us, no wonder the scriptures repeatedly describe "men's hearts failing them for fear" (Luke

21:26, Moses 7:66). Despite all the negative press about conditions in today's society, there is a way to survive it all; there is a way to be free from the depressing and frightening negativism of so much terror and violence. Jesus said, "I am the way, the truth and the life" (D. Kelly Ogden, *Optimism in a Time of Terror*).

Many in our day will seek God, and some will determine to find Christ, but we realize no one can come to the Father unless they fully receive His Son. We are totally dependent upon Christ. No one can circumvent the appointed Savior of our Heavenly Father's system.

> Let me clarify a distinguishing characteristic about your identity. You are the children who God chose to be part of his battalion during this great climax in the long-standing battle between good and evil, between truth and error. (President Nelson, *BYU Devotional*, 9/17/19)

Pres. Nelson continues,

> There are extraordinary young people and devoted Christians throughout the world willing to take up the cause to stand firm in the last days. Research and cultural experts have labeled this generation as millennials, and they present a somewhat negative view of the behavior of the upcoming generation. However, I have asked the Lord about you, the modern-day millennials. The spiritual impression tells me that the term millennials may be a perfect term for you, for much different reasons the experts may never understand. "Millennial" can remind you of who you really are and what your purpose really is. In the premortal world, you understood the Gospel, you kept your first estate and made covenants with Heavenly Father. There are courageous, even morally courageous, things that you would

do while here on earth. You are "true" millenni-
als, men and women whom God trusted to send
forth during the most compelling dispensation
of the history of the world. Learn who you really
are. You are an elect son or daughter of God.
You are created in His image. You were taught
and prepared for anything and everything you
will face. Expect and prepare to accomplish the
impossible.

Our Savior and Redeemer, Jesus Christ, will
perform some of His mightiest works between
now and when He comes again. We will see
miraculous indications that God the Father and
His Son, Jesus Christ, preside over this world
in majesty and glory. But in the coming days, it
will not be possible to survive spiritually without
the guiding, directing, comforting, and constant
influence of the Holy Ghost. A man or woman
living now can help prepare the earth for the second coming of Jesus Christ for His millennial
reign. (Russell M. Nelson)

God's children are weighted and wired for spiritual success. The
desire to reach for God and acquire power over death is inherent in
all people and cultures. True doctrines and ordinances of the Gospel
of Christ fortify faith and give hope in His return.

Spiritual development and power comes to those who are prepared and willing to stand with Christ, and under the most challenging circumstances, will survive, whether in life or death.

This quote comes from *Resource*, Jeffrey Bradshaw, pp. 171–172:

The continual challenge endemic in a disci-
ple's life should teach us something about standing, itself. Namely, what may appear as a static
position, will, with experience be understood as
a point of equilibrium or balance in the eye of a

storm. Lest anyone think living life continually standing in the presence of God is a heavy, humdrum safe affair I give you a quote from G.K. Chesterton who understood the essence of discipleship is to maintain the equilibrium of a man behind madly rushing horses, seeming to swoop this way and to sway that way yet, in every attitude having the grace of statuary and the accuracy of arithmetic. It is always simple to fall; there is infinity of angles in which one falls, but only one at which one stands! (From the book, *Orthodoxy*, pp. 102–1108)

It seems to me a fool's bargain to reject the Gospel of Jesus Christ containing God's great saving plan. Christ intends to elevate us to be better than we are now. You and I need to quiet our fears and develop a full trust in Him. Faith comes before miracles, and our prayers of gratitude are the greatest tool of receivership from God.

Pres. Nelson reveals an opinion, "I am not naive about the days ahead. We live in a world that is complex and increasingly contentious. The constant availability of social media, and a twenty-four-hour news cycle bombard us with relentless messages. If we are to have any hope of sifting through the myriad of voices and the philosophies of men that attack truth, we must learn to receive revelation."

Having searched end-time bible prophecy, one would be remiss in failing to clearly state the unvarnished truth of what has been prophesied regarding our days. Our times are the end-time of the earth as we know it. Many of the world populations will not survive the variety and intensity of the coming events. There will be an increasing perfect storm of many cataclysmic events in all parts of the world. The odds of escaping are unlikely.

It is also possible that there will be martyrs in our future. Beloved church leaders, ministers, and lay members of all Christian congregations throughout the world may seal their testimonies with their blood.

Practicing faithful Christians are not immune to a growing prejudice spreading itself in the United States. Dallin Oaks, a current leader in the Church of Jesus Christ of Latter-day Saints, specifies the dilemma.

> Christians look to God for standards of behavior. These laws of God regulate our moral structure and obedience to his truth. The diluted laws put in place through political and social pressures cannot override adherence to the higher standard laws of God. Some institutions can change their policy and perhaps even their doctrines. We cannot and would not. Our doctrines are vouchsafed in God's plan for all of us. We cannot be compelled to cast aside truth for deteriorating moral standards because they are embraced by a majority. A majority vote does not change eternal moral principles. Our entrenched standard may summon the wild dogs of persecution. We may find an invasion of the free exercise of our religion. We may be labeled bigots, haters, prejudiced and self-righteous by our detractors. We must never dilute our priority to trust in and follow God's plan. Never deviate from the goals set by God to return clean and worthy and obedient to His presence.

We must look to Christ and adhere to this challenge. "And ye shall be hated of all men for my name's sake; but he that endureth to the end shall be saved" (Matt. 10:22).

These will be times like no other. The world will deal with pervasive diseases and illnesses, famines, destructive weather events like howling storms, winds, wildfires, tsunamis, and flooding. There will be wars and disputes between countries leading to a world war.

The Armageddon War will usher in the Second Coming of Christ, but take heart in this message:

> A thousand shall fall at thy side, and ten thousand at thy right hand; but it shall not come nigh thee. Because thou hast made the Lord, which is my refuge, even the most High thy habitation; there shall no evil befall thee, neither shall any plague come nigh thy dwelling. For he shall give his angels charge over thee, to keep thee in all thy ways. They shall bear thee up in their hands lest thou dash thy foot against a stone. (Ps. 91:7–11)

These horrific events are clearly outlined in Revelation 6.

> And I beheld when he had opened the *sixth seal, and, lo, there was a great *earthquake; and the *sun became *black as sackcloth of hair, and the moon became as *blood; And the stars of heaven fell unto the earth, even as a fig tree casteth her *untimely figs, when she is shaken of a mighty wind. *And the heaven departed as a *scroll when it is rolled together; and every *mountain and island were moved out of their places. And the *kings of the earth, and the great men, and the rich men, and the chief captains, and the mighty men, and every bondman, and every free man, hid themselves in the *dens and in the rocks of the mountains; And said to the *mountains and rocks, Fall on us, and hide us from the face of him that sitteth on the throne, and from the wrath of the Lamb:For the great *day of his wrath is come; and who shall be able to *stand? (Rev. 6:12–16)

Christians will be able to stand, waiting upon the Lord to come. We must be loyal and fearless.

> The Lord is my light and my salvation; whom shall I fear? The Lord is the strength of my life, of whom shall I be afraid? When the wicked, even mine enemies and my foes come upon me to eat my flesh, they stumbled and fell... For in the time of trouble He shall hide me in His pavilion in the secret of His tabernacle shall He hide me. He shall set me upon a rock... Wait on the Lord be of good courage and He shall strengthen thine heart; wait I say on the Lord. (Ps. 27:1–2, 5, 14)

Devoted Christians over a lifetime can come to know the gospel is not only true, but also it works. It works today as it worked for our ancient bible prophets and early Christians. In fact, as true Christians, we have the latent personal revelation powers to manifest blessings, see visions, and receive ministering of angels because we are the children of God.

Ancient prophets saw and anticipated our very day. These are exciting and exhilarating times. The fuller blessings may be ours in spite of the underlying challenges. Perhaps it is fortunate that we live in the fullness of time and the fast-approaching premillennial age. Some of us may participate in the glorious Second Coming of the Savior.

> We cannot choose how long our earth experience will be, we cannot reckon God's long range time-table, or control the world events of our day; but we can choose to bring our private lives into harmony with the Plan of happiness provided by our Father. (Neal Maxwell)

Could it be that some might be spiritually reinforced and upgraded for this day? "And it shall come to pass afterward, *that* I will pour out my spirit upon all flesh; and your sons and your daughters shall prophesy, your old men shall dream dreams, your young men shall see visions and also upon the servants and upon the handmaids in those days will I pour out my spirit" (Joel 2:28).

Apostle Neil A. Anderson states that a compensatory power is possible for some. "The Lord has long anticipated this important period of human history. He knows the end from the beginning. The Savior has assured us in our day, 'Be of good cheer, and do not fear, for I the Lord am with you, and will stand by you.'"

As we find our way in a world less attentive to the commandments of God, we will certainly be prayerful, but we need not be overly alarmed. The Lord will bless His saints with the added spiritual power necessary to meet the challenges of our day. Here is my major theme this morning: As evil increases in the world, there is a compensatory spiritual power for the righteous. As the world slides from its spiritual moorings, the Lord prepares the way for those who seek Him, offering them greater assurance, greater confirmation, and greater confidence in the spiritual direction they are traveling. The power of the Holy Ghost becomes a brighter light in the emerging twilight.

John Pontius, from his book *Approaching Zion*, stated:

> Nothing is withheld from our grasp. It is necessary we put our faith into operation. This spiritual attunement comes at a personal price. It requires strict adherence to the laws of God. It requires one to become anchored and saturated in the purifying characteristics of people worthy of Zion. The once held vision of Zion was commonly understood, but then seems to have become lost. There has been a collective forgetfulness of how the pure in heart are formed. We are scarcely cognizant of our privileges regarding Zion. We are like children playing in a sandbox filled with diamonds; we have played in them so long that we esteem them merely as sparkling sand.

The Bible reveals the whole city of Enoch, and the ancient residents of the city of Melchizedek were translated. Their home became the habitation of translated beings enjoying the glorified environment of the city of Zion, a place prepared especially for them off this earth.

Moses, Elijah, and John the Beloved were also translated. Translation is not a permanent state but an intermediate condition prior to resurrection. Translated bodies are designed for future missions. Moses and Elijah had future missions. They appeared with Christ on the mount of transfiguration. They and John have future missions relating to our day.

I would refer you to, 3 Nephi 28 in the *Book of Mormon*, which gives the most detailed scriptural account of the doctrine of translation than any other scripture. Alma, Nephi, and Ether were translated. (See Alma 45:18–19; 3 Nephi 1:2–3, 2:9; Ether 15:34.)

Some men and women will be upgraded, enhanced, and perfectly suited for the days ahead. Individuals will be prepared by God. They will be "added upon," receiving gifts, powers, and life-enhancing abilities. They will set about to fulfill millennial ministries for the purpose of protecting and assisting those who survive the destruction. A good portion of the world inhabitants will survive the chaotic disturbances in the earth and escape the burning. Some of those may become translated beings.

Translated Beings

Translation is a quickening or spiritual transformation of the body. This upgrade is endowed by the power of God bringing a person from a lower to a higher power state in which they can be in the presence of deity yet still interact with and participate in the mortal realm. Others will not necessarily recognize the translated beings among them.

God holds all power that ultimately quickens His creations and increases the glory of an entity or an identity depending upon which portion of the power spectrum one attunes to. This glorified change brought upon mortals protects them from the effects of illness, death, exhaustion, hunger and enhances one's abilities to move about, relocate, and transport oneself quickly. Once their translation ministries are completed, a transformation takes place. A form of death experience will be a simple crossing over in a "twinkling" from a translated state to the final state of resurrection.

During the millennium, the righteous and translated beings will share this regenerated and glorified earth we live on now. They can and do interact with mortals often without recognition. Translated beings will appear just like normal mortals.

All the righteous translated beings and mortals that survive the burning will be the grateful congregation who spend the thousand-year millennium with our Savior. They can look forward to this glorious transitioning process at the Second Coming of Christ.

Science fact: Step up attraction principles apply in science. Small energetic entities move in step fashion toward higher energized objects that tend to draw them like magnets.

Christ expands this concept on a grander scale, as we read in 3 Nephi 27:14, "And my father sent me that I might be lifted up upon the cross: and after that I had been lifted up upon the cross, that I might draw all men unto me, that as I have been lifted up by men even so should men be lifted up by the Father, to stand before me, to be judged of their works, whether they be good or whether they be evil."

Those who survive the final burning will be drawn like magnets to Christ and live with Him on a cleansed more energized earth through thousand years of peace. This same scientific principle will be in operation at the end of the millennium when the earth undergoes its final upgrade and humans undergo the final judgment. The righteous will receive glorified resurrected bodies by which they are able to accommodate the additional glory and power upgrade of earth. The renewed earth and righteous renewed men and women will become residents of God's dominion for eternity.

After this I beheld, and, lo, a great multitude, which no man could number, of all nations, and ᵃkindreds, and people, and tongues, stood before the throne, and before the Lamb, clothed with white robes, and ᵇpalms in their hands… And one of the elders answered, saying unto me, What are these which are arrayed in white robes? and whence came they? And I said unto him, Sir, thou knowest. And he said to me, These are they which came ᵃout of great ᵇtribulation, and have ᶜwashed their robes, and made them ᵈwhite in the ᵉblood of the ᶠLamb. Therefore are they before the throne of God, and serve him day and night in his ᵃtemple: and he that ᵇsitteth on the throne shall ᶜdwell among them… For the Lamb which is in the midst of the throne shall feed them, and shall lead them unto living fountains of ᵃwaters: and God shall wipe away all ᵇtears from their eyes. (Rev. 7:9, 13–15, 17)

Carol Lynn Pearson in her poem, "Provision for the End," gives us a holy directive.

> What to do when
> The dawn brings night
> And the moon spins out
> And the stars fall white?
> Wait calm in the silence
> The black sky spilled:
> Your lamp will light
> If it is filled.

"You are children of the light. Fill your lamps."

About the Author

Juanita Collard Werrett is an author, writer, poet, teacher, and, most significantly, a lifelong student and researcher. Her areas of interest are the study of science and the Gospel of Jesus Christ.

She has taught Bible studies and the life of Christ regularly over the past forty years for her church. She has taught individual students in her home for the past ten years as they sought understanding of truths found in Scriptures.

In 2015, she committed herself to a rigorous internet curriculum taught by scientist, Anthony Patch. She absorbed his knowledge of particle physics, quantum computers, and futuristic technology. The rich experience of that interaction led to the remarkable content of this published volume. The supportive platform of science lends itself to the spiritual platforms of God. An understanding of this concept became life changing. She is offering this experience to others.

Her personal student curriculums are self-imposed, consistent over her lifetime, and continue today. She is one of that great population called seekers. She feels learning must not only inform but also transform the student.

She continues to interlace her academic and religious studies through her primary life as a dedicated wife and mother of four wonderful children.

CPSIA information can be obtained
at www.ICGtesting.com
Printed in the USA
BVHW081957151221
624018BV00005B/576

9 781098 069650